Emily Ros

MW00697923

BREAK
the
GLASS
SLIPPER

Embrace Your
Inner Queen!

Christy Becker

Disclaimer:

This book contains personal stories of past clients.
Some names have been changed.

ISBN: 978-0-578-59030-1

Edited by: Mariah Sage

BREAK *the* GLASS SLIPPER

FREE YOURSELF FROM FAIRY TALE FANTASIES AND FIND TRUE LOVE IN REAL LIFE

CRISTA BECK

Contents

For

Jean

Once upon a time...

"Oh, wow! This feels like a movie."

I'll never forget the day Ethan opened up the large glass shower door, walked in fully clothed and held me under the warm stream of water.

I cried. Not only because I was hurt by what he had just said to me moments before, but because it was such a beautiful and surreal moment to be held by a strong, handsome man in such a dramatic and romantic way. Through my tears I kept thinking to myself, "This feels like a movie" over and over again.

It didn't seem real, even though it was.

Or was it?

My name is Crista Beck and I help single people find love again. Over the past 10+ years I have led people in the area of love and relationships. You may have seen me on TV news shows or on the TEDx stage as a featured guest and expert. My message has served over a million people around the world.

My clients are successful six- and seven-figure professionals who have everything going for them in their lives. They have the house, the car, the great career, the money, and great friends and family. They have everything... except love. They come to me when they aren't meeting people who are successful or intelligent enough, when they're tired of the inauthenticity of dating apps, and they think dating feels like work. But what they really want is to find a real connection with a quality person that has long-term potential.

Take Brittany who was tired of all the disappearing men she encountered in the dating scene. I helped her find the love of her life (in just a few months). Within a year after that she was engaged and then married.

I helped Maya heal from her painful divorce and learn to listen to her own inner voice. Within months, she found a grounded and family-oriented man who cared for her deeply. They have merged lives and own a home together now.

I helped Marc, who came to me when his love life felt empty and lonely. Within months he found the woman of his dreams and started planning a romantic ski getaway to France with this beautiful woman. Fast forward to a year later and he got down on one knee and she said, "Yes!".

This is the kind of magic that I get to be a part of.

I find my work to be deeply fulfilling. My life feels so blessed, happy, and full.

But it wasn't always this way...

I had first met Ethan on OkCupid. The only opportunity we had to meet up in person was after one of my Bikram yoga classes. I warned him that I was going to be sweaty and that my hair would be up in a messy bun. If he wanted to meet me that way, I could meet him at Summermoon Coffee at 7 p.m. He was in. He turned out to be a great conversationalist. We laughed and played. And even though I noticed that it seemed like he was competing with me, I laughed it off. Everything I said, he would say something to top me. I disregarded it because it was all just fun and games. I seriously thought he was one of the most handsome men I've ever been on a date with. At the end of our first date he asked me out again. I immediately said yes.

We went out to a little French place with beautiful lighting and ambiance. We sat across from each other and joyously connected, and then this happened:

He stood up from his seat, sat down right next to me on the elegantly cushioned bench, and whispered in my ear, "It looks like you need to be kissed" and proceeded to kiss me so tenderly and completely – right in the middle of the restaurant.

I thought to myself, "This feels like a movie."

From there the romantic film of our relationship began.

And it was my kind of movie – filled with romantic moments, grand gestures, ear whispers, and love letters. Every woman's dream. And especially MY dream, to be adored and appreciated in this most magical way.

So even though a red flag went up when he told me that he still owned a home with a girlfriend he only dated for a year, I swept it under the rug and enjoyed the thousand-dollar shopping spree he gave me at my favorite boutique. When he told me that he divorced his ex-wife because she was crazy, I ignored the fact that I personally hate it when men call women crazy because I know that's just a way men diminish women's feelings. So instead, I squealed with delight when he left me flowers and a romantic card on the dining room table before he left for a business trip.

A year into the relationship, it got hard to ignore the strange feeling I felt inside my body when he would leave each week, traveling for work. You see, I'm a woman who is very comfortable and at ease with my alone time and I love my independent life, so when I started to feel insecure when he left, it didn't make much sense.

This "insecure feeling" popped up again, but because he took me on a romantic trip to see the band that played my favorite romantic song, I disregarded it. There I was at this intimate venue, listening live to a song that always deeply warmed my heart, and I was holding this handsome man's hand as tears flowed from my face because the moment was so overwhelmingly beautiful.

I ignored the sinking feeling in my heart again because he brought thoughtful gifts when he came to meet my family for the first time. He wanted to impress them, and this delighted my heart because now, it was getting serious, and I relished in that.

But none of these romantic gestures made that "insecure" or "something is off" feeling go away.

Over time, this started to disturb me greatly, so as any healthy person would do when they were struggling with a mental/ emotional issue, I sought out a therapist to talk it through. I shared the experience I was having with Ethan and he recommended a therapist he had used years ago when he was going through his divorce. He said, "Diane was great!" I called her up, told her that Ethan recommended me and with a soft, and yet urgent voice, she said, "Come in immediately."

Between scheduling the initial appointment and actually meeting with Diane, multiple tragic events unfolded, but to sum it up, Ethan went out one night and never came home. I called him multiple times that evening worried sick and got no response. When I called him the next morning, he said he was out with a friend all night and stayed at a hotel. He even got annoyed with me for calling him. I thought to myself, "Something is not right here."

At that moment I realized that it was time to trust my gut, take this event as a major sign to take my things and leave. And then I waited. I waited for a phone call. I waited for an apology. I waited, for something, anything.

But nothing.

I experienced being ghosted in the ultimate sense. One minute I was in what I thought was a wonderfully romantic relationship filled with unforgettable moments, and the next minute he was completely gone. Radio silence.

"You dodged a bullet."

This was one of the first things Diane said to me when I showed up to my appointment.

I'll never forget being in her leather furniture filled office when she braced me for some of the worst news I would ever receive in my life. By telling me what she was about to tell me, she was borderline risking her psychology license because as a therapist, she promises to uphold certain levels of conduct. One of those rules is to not reveal confidential information, including facts or data about a client to a third party. What she told me altered my reality forever.

"Ethan is not who you think he is."

My heart started pounding so loudly I could hear it in my ears. I felt the room start to slowly spin as Diane's voice got super crisp and slow.

"Because I have to honor my confidentiality as a therapist, I cannot tell you any details. You are such a bright light and I don't want you to think any of this is your fault."

I thought to myself, "Wait. What?"

"What are you talking about?"

"Nothing that happened is your fault. You didn't do anything wrong. Ethan is the kind of man that is an expert at deception and lives a double life. He will never change. That is all I can tell you."

Wait. What? My reality starting to crash down around me. All of the tender kisses, the trips, the cards, the flowers, all started to crash down around me as a lie. I felt like my brain was cracking into a million pieces. And then Diane continued, "If you want to know who he really is, then read *People of the Lie*. That's all I can tell you."

I was shaken to the core when I left Diane's office that day, but a huge seed had been planted in my mind.

The answer to all of my questions were supposedly located in a book on a shelf in a used bookstore. When I entered Half Price Books on South Lamar, I experienced that same thought again, but this time I felt like I was in a strange thriller film.

"This feels like a movie."

Instead of feelings of butterflies and romance, now the experience was one of terror.

I bought the book, drove home, tucked myself into bed, and opened up the front cover. It was a hard read, not because of complicated language, but because it was dark subject matter.

It was extremely unsettling because if what Diane said was

true, I had been in a relationship with someone who was a pathological liar. The words in this book meant that his goal in our relationship was to win, and by "win," I mean his goal was to emotionally manipulate me. His goal was to chip away at my self-worth in a subtle way so I would get to the point of thinking everything was my fault. (I even thought the insecure feelings I had experienced were my fault and something I needed to fix about myself, instead of me relating to my powerful intuition as something that guides and protects me).

It was devastating to read that there are human beings out there that are truly soul-killers, people who want to murder your spirit and self-worth, but it was impossible for Ethan to kill my spirit. I was way too strong. I was way too secure with myself. I was way too loved by my friends and family. When he couldn't win, he left. He couldn't conquer me.

And even though I am a strong and resilient woman, this experience of having the rug pulled out from beneath me, and realizing that the relationship was a complete lie, left me completely devastated. This was paradigm altering for me because I had lived in a reality that all people were beautiful and good. My friends even jokingly called me a Care Bear because of my precious focus on sending love into the world.

There are moments in life that will change you...forever.

And this experience forced me to take a deep, hard look at how I got into this situation.

"How did I not see? How did this happen to me?"

I thought love was supposed to feel like a movie. I thought romance meant true love. I had bought into the fairy tales that were pumped into my system starting from a young tender age, sitting in front of the TV watching Disney films. I put romance on a pedestal above all else and because of this, I was easy prey for someone like Ethan. He knew all the things he needed to do to trap a woman like me. I bought into the fairy tale that Prince Charming was going to whisk me away and sweep me off my feet.

And that's exactly what happened. I was swept off my feet and into a Cinderella dream, but was pushed out of the magic carriage at midnight only to be left flat on my face in the mud.

It wasn't until I realized that the fairy tales I had bought into were what caused my suffering. Only then was I able to shift.

And that's why I'm so passionate about helping single people distinguish their own fairy tales that get in the way of having the partner they truly desire. This book is designed to free you from the fairy tale fantasies so you can find true love in real life.

Are you curious to know what your fairy tales may be?

We all have them. You can't live in our culture without having at least one to contend with. To start, let me define for you what I consider a fairy tale.

Definition of a fairy tale: a fabricated story, especially one intended to deceive.

In terms of your love life, a fairy tale is a made-up story propagated by our society through film, TV, and advertising. These stories have been taken up in our culture as the truth and are shared as acceptable messages. You may even hear your friends and family, who love you dearly and only want the best for you, tell you these fairy tales about love. But these fairy tales are false and are getting in the way of us creating a realistic roadmap to finding love.

They become a part of our thinking and decision-making process when it comes to dating, relationships and romantic love.

They can constrain us. Just by believing them, we are prevented from seeing reality. They even show up as limiting beliefs about ourselves and our self-identity. These fairy tales may also be about other people and the world in general. When undistinguished, we will be forever under their magic spell, which will prevent us from having the love we sincerely desire.

My mission in life, and in this book, is to help you distinguish what your own personal fairy tales are and to kick them to the curb. Because in the end, they're just made-up stories that are not true.

Each chapter in this book highlights the top ten fairy tales that I have come across over and over again in my years as a dating expert and coach. My intention with this book is to expose these fairy tales in broad daylight, because once you see them, you can't unsee them. That's the point of this book. To have you see, with your own two beautiful eyes, the stories that have been holding you back from creating a reality-based relationship that has long-term potential.

This book is for you if you're ready for a relationship but for some reason love just hasn't happened for you yet. If you are ready to grow and take a deep look at yourself and the potential impact your own fairy tales are having on your own love life, you are in for something eye-opening and potentially even life changing.

This is not for you if you don't want to look at your choices in life. I am very clearly going to show you how you may be getting in your own way in creating the love you desire. If you're not willing to take responsibility for your part in how your love life has gone, this book is not for you.

But if you are ready to break your own glass slipper, I jam-packed this book with tools and techniques to free yourself of your own self-created reality that is most likely holding you back from experiencing the love of your life.

Time to get your sledgehammer out, and let's get smashing....

The Poisonous Apple and the Dating Coma

"Love Will Just Magically Happen...When You Least Expect It"

The Evil Queen misleads Snow White into eating the poisonous apple, which places a spell over her and puts her into a never-ending deep sleep... Similarly, Hollywood romantic comedies have misled single women and placed them into a dating coma, by force feeding the fairy tale: Love magically happens when you least expect it!

Accidental meetings happen all the time in Hollywood films, so we've been conditioned to think this is a normal and *expected* occurrence. We think love is actually supposed to happen this way. Take, for example, the cute and random first meeting of William and Anna from *Notting Hill*.

William Thacker, played by Hugh Grant, is an unsuccessful Notting Hill bookstore owner. One day, Anna Scott, played by

Julia Roberts, the world's most famous and beautiful actress, enters his shop. A day or two later, William surprisingly runs into her again – this time bumping into her on the street and spilling a cup of orange juice all over her white shirt. Anna accepts his offer to change in his nearby apartment, and thanks him with a kiss goodbye. Love ensues from there.

We eat this stuff up as if it were a large bowl of delicious mashed potatoes after a bad day at work, but if this were *real* life, it might look a little bit more like this…

You walk into a bookstore, shop around a bit, and bring your paperback copy of *50 Shades of Gray* to the checkout counter in the most discrete fashion possible. (It's that same feeling you have when you bring that box of condoms to the cashier.) Despite the awkwardness, you bravely pull out your credit card to buy it because you figure it's about time you see what all of the fuss is about. The book is always better than the movies, right? You're going to see for yourself this time.

Because you are disoriented by your own slight embarrassment and the random text message you just received, you barely notice that the bookstore owner is cute and thinks you're attractive. He does his best to flirt a little, but it doesn't even show up on your radar that he is interested. You fail to notice this potential opportunity to find love, so you leave, say thank you, and walk out the door.

The next day, you are walking down the street, and you bump into that same guy. You don't even recognize him from yesterday. He spills orange juice all over you. This "stranger" encourages you to come back to his apartment to change. You kindly say, "No, thank you," run back home, take a shower, put your pajamas on, pick up where you left off in *50 Shades of Gray*, and you never see him again.

This is what would happen, at best, if we were to place you or any other woman in this circumstance.

Yet, in our culture, we have a belief that we'll magically meet our true love in a random manner, without any effort on our part.

This belief has permeated our society.

To think that Prince Charming is just going to come knocking on your door is not only highly unlikely, but it's a Hollywood fantasy. And as intelligent, modern women, it's time for us to stop buying into it.

BEWARE: HOLLYWOOD IS POISONING YOUR LOVE LIFE

Hollywood romantic comedies are designed to put the "fantasy" in romance. Have you ever been on a date that takes place on a magical carpet, riding through the stars and stopping off at various famous landmarks around the world? If so, you were either on drugs, or deep in REM sleep. The whole purpose of the movies is the fun of entering a world where dreams come true and happily ever afters happen every day.

We watch these movies when we need some warm fuzzies, to escape, and feel good.

The problem is, unless you have lived in the woods your entire life, you've probably watched hundreds of movies in your lifetime. Based on an article in USA Today, an average American will watch over 5000 films in their lifetime. That's about 365 days of nonstop viewing!

These films, like *Notting Hill*, influence the way we see the world and play a huge part in our beliefs and expectations in romance, love, and relationships.

In fact, we are inundated with this perspective from media, advertising and even our family and friends.

You may have even had a loving Auntie tell you after your last break up, "Don't worry sweetie, love's just going to happen for you."

Your friends and family mean well, but this kind of

encouragement may be feeding an underlying belief that there is absolutely nothing you need to do to find a quality life partner. There is no action, no strategy, and no effort necessary.

Believing this fairy tale will get you nowhere. It will keep you in the *fantasy* of dating instead of *reality*. It's time to run the Evil Queen off the top of the mountain just like the Seven Dwarfs did.

If you were raised watching Disney, you've seen the magic moment many times… there were cartoon hearts, birds, and rainbows coming out of their eyes when they fell in love instantaneously (and out of the blue, of course!). No wonder you think each and every date you go on is Boringsville. No wonder you are disappointed with your love life.

Over and over again, I hear single women say they don't meet any men with whom they feel a spark. The expectation is for an instant love connection. The expectation is the hearts, birds and rainbows, and when these are not present, they think it wasn't meant to be.

If you find yourself clinging on to this fantasy, the poisonous apple that you've bitten into from Hollywood needs to be thrown into the trash.

How is love going to happen when you get up in the morning,

drive to work, work all day, drive home, workout, take a shower, get in your PJs and watch Netflix the rest of the night?

Love is not going to happen if you don't create opportunities for love to happen.

Take Sasha, for example. She was a 38-year-old single woman who had never married, went to church each and every week, had a great group of friends, a wonderful family, and a great career. She truly believed that love was going to happen for her.

DVDs of tender-hearted rom coms filled the shelves of her living room like Ever After, Leap Year, and Titanic. She also had many Hallmark movies crammed onto that shelf and had watched some of these DVDs 5-8 times.

On the outside, her words spoke mostly of hope. When asked about her love life she would say the same words over and over again, "I will meet him when the timing is right...I'm praying about it...When it's ready to happen, it will happen."

But if you were to take a peek into this woman's love and dating life you would see that it was non-existent. There were no dates. No singles' groups. No blind dates. No online dating. Nothing. She took absolutely no action. She truly believed that love was just going to happen without her having to make any changes to her current behavior.

But deep down, she was lonely. She felt the pain of going to bed alone at night. She thought something was wrong with her because she had not found her husband yet. She thought, "Love has happened for all my other friends. They're all getting married, so why has it not happened for me? I really thought I would have met him by now."

After over a decade as a dating coach, I couldn't even count how many times I've heard, "I really thought it would have happened by now."

This is the downside to subconsciously believing the fairy tale that love will magically happen. You think it WILL just happen, all on its own, so you focus on your career, your friends, your hobbies, but you don't focus on creating *movement and opportunities* in your love life. You have a great life, but you don't have someone to share it with.

How are you going to meet the man of your dreams if you are not putting yourself out there? How are you going to have the intimacy you deeply crave if you are staying home every night? How are you going to have the security of a loving partnership if you're not meeting any new single people?

Believing this fairy tale lets you off the hook from being responsible for doing anything about it.

Love doesn't just happen when you're sitting on the couch, period.

If that were true, then your only chance to meet someone new would be the pizza delivery guy or the plumber!

This kind of "magical" thinking is unconsciously sabotaging the love life of floods of people who are scared to death that they are not going to find a happy, enduring relationship! They toss and turn at night fearful that love won't happen for them.

Take Cara, for example. I was on one of my initial intro calls with her and she said, "I have a great personality. I'm fun and cute. What am I not doing right? I'm not attracting anyone right now and this really scares me."

She thought something was wrong with her.

When I asked her, "How many dates do you go on per month?"

She said, "Zero."

When I probed a little deeper to see if I could get a clearer snapshot of her love life, what we discovered is that she was spending less than an hour a month creating opportunities for a relationship to happen.

There was an ah-ha moment on the call where everything

clicked for her. Instead of thinking that her lack of a love life was due to personal shortcomings, she realized it was because she was not taking any action.

She thought a man was just going to magically manifest himself. But in reality, she didn't place her dating life as a priority and was not making any effort at all.

You absolutely need to get out there, away from your comfort zone (in baby steps!) and create love to happen for you.

Remember Sasha from earlier, the 38-year-old woman who has never married and thought love would just happen? Well, let me tell you how this story ends.

Her father was worried about her and was trying to help her find a nice man. Through friends, her dad found a man that could be a good fit for her and encouraged her to meet him for coffee. Sasha did meet him, but reluctantly. She wanted nothing to do with this man her dad set her up with, but somehow, that initial meeting acted like a fire underneath her.

You see, she had been crushing on a guy at church for over a year. Each time she saw him, she would get all happy inside, but she never approached him. Within that same week of having coffee with that other man, she sat next to her crush at church, introduced herself, and he asked her out for coffee. Fast forward, he proposed within 6 months and they are currently married. All it took was for her to do something other than her normal default behavior.

Now it's your turn!

 BREAK THE GLASS SLIPPER FOR
"WHEN YOU LEAST EXPECT IT, LOVE WILL JUST HAPPEN."

How do you break out of the bonds of this particular fairy tale fantasy?

Believing that love is just going to happen is more poisonous than the apple the Evil Queen gave to Snow White.

Consciously and consistently being the Ruler of your own love life is the only antidote.

To flourish inside the process of dating one must be purposeful just like the ruler of a kingdom. A benevolent and effective queen does not leave things by chance. She is solely responsible for the success or failure of her kingdom.

Place it in modern terms, a CEO is accountable for the goals and vision for the company and she has definiteness of purpose and clearness of view. Her level of predetermination is potent.

Just like the CEO is clearly and solidly stepping into the possibility of growth and financial success for her company, you are stepping into the possibility of life-long love.

You are no longer going to approach your journey from a fairy tale illusion, but as the captain of your own ship, steering your beautiful yacht into the port of the stability of a genuine and grounded relationship.

The CEO doesn't just hope that the company succeeds, the CEO creates the momentum necessary to make sure it succeeds.

Real magic happens when you are in action.

It's time to kick this fairy tale to the curb and reclaim your power. No more putting the success of your love life in the hands of some made-up story!

Love is not something that happens *outside* of you. You have the power to create love to happen.

You have the power to go out and meet new people. You have the power to go and join singles groups that are in alignment with what you enjoy and like in life. Only you can choose to talk to your friends and family about this specific kind of partner you're looking for. You can go online and sort through some profiles and go on some dates with some quality men.

You get to create your love life and your dating life to go how you want it to go.

Love isn't just going to happen *out there*. It happens with you by its side. It happens with you making your love life a priority and taking actions in alignment with that.

******

EXERCISE:

Dating is the gateway to marriage and a lifelong partnership. Taking actions in alignment with meeting new single people, going out on dates with quality potential partners, and sorting them based on your vision for your life is key.

First, examine the current landscape of your dating life. Grab a journal and answer the following questions: How many people are you currently dating? How many dates have you been on in the past 30 days? How many new single people do you meet per week on average? How much time are you currently spending on your dating life per week?

It's very important to look at what is happening *in reality* with your love life. What do you see from taking this snapshot?

What new actions can you begin to take?

CHAPTER RECAP:

- You are not going to meet your true love while sitting on the couch watching Netflix.
- Stay open to and create opportunities to have love happen.
- Take consistent daily actions to regularly meet new single people, go out on dates, and ultimately you will meet, "The One."

Now you know that believing the fairy tale, "love will just magically happen", is just a way to avoid taking full responsibility for your love life. With this knowledge you can now make the choice to take small actions that will create the compound effect to have the loving relationship you deeply desire.

It's time now to see how to create a powerful connection with a man, but it may look totally different than you think. If you're stuck in this next fairy tale, it could potentially have you miss out on your one true love...

2.

The Problem with Prince Charming

"I'll Know Him When I Meet Him"

There's a reason why Queen Elsa from "Frozen" said, "No" when Princess Anna asked for her blessing to marry Prince Hans. True love isn't something that happens in an instant or throughout the duration of an onscreen duet. So, where does it happen?

"Love is a lot like the movies," said no one, ever.

But do you know what many single women actually believe? They believe that when they meet a man on a first date they will just *know* if he is the right man for them. Countless women think that if a man sweeps them off their feet early on, it's a true sign that he's the one.

This belief in "love at first sight" has not only permeated

Hollywood and Disney films alike but has infiltrated how we choose potential partners to date.

Take the Hollywood classic romantic comedy, *Serendipity*, where Jonathan and Sara meet while grabbing for the last pair of cashmere gloves while shopping at Bloomingdales in New York City. Despite each being in a relationship with other people at the time, the magic was right, and a night of Christmas shopping turned into romance. Even though it was a "love at first sight" moment, realizing they were both in committed relationships, they choose to part ways... but not before giving fate a chance to prove they're truly meant to be together. Love at first sight wins, they finally meet again, and the ending of the film insinuates that they live happily ever after (even though they only met once, many years before and only spent a few hours together!)

This belief in "love at first sight" has led many single people to think that if they don't have a magical, knock your socks off moment with someone, then it is not meant to be.

Here's the classic formula of many fairy tales:

Once upon a time, a beautiful young princess set eyes on a handsome prince. Their *connection is instant*, and they fall in love mid-song, as princes and princesses so often do. But wait, not so fast. Something threatening comes along to tear this perfect couple apart for eternity. It's ok though. True love eventually prevails, sealed with a kiss and they live happily ever after. The end.

> *"Our mental synchronization can have but ONE explanation, you and I were just meant to be."*
> - Hans and Anna from Frozen

Here's the part of this classic formula that I want to draw your attention to: "Their connection was instant."

When you believe the fairy tale of instant connection, you don't even realize how many *opportunities* for true love you miss out on. That's the dark and disturbing side of this fairy tale. You're so firmly rooted in your belief that the *right* man will sweep you off your feet... so when you meet a new guy and there aren't immediate sparks, you write him off. And without knowing it, you miss out on someone who could have been a wonderful lifelong partner for you.

LOST OPPORTUNITIES

Here's an actual word for word (no editing) email to me from one of my clients after she just started working with me (look closely at the words she uses):

"I went out on a date last night. We had a pleasant time together, but there were no fireworks. Nothing was off the charts. There was some chemistry, but it was not boiling over. He was nice. I think he liked me. But, Crista, I wasn't blown away by him. What should I do? He didn't really sweep me off my feet. I really didn't "feel it" with him. I really didn't feel like he was going to be my future husband. I just can't see it."

Then she sent me the screenshot of what she texted him:

"Hey, it was really nice meeting you. I just don't think we're a good fit. Good luck."

Gulp was my internal response.

Many people think that when they show up on a first date, they should just have "that feeling." If they don't, they immediately say, "Adios."

"HE WILL JUST SWEEP ME OFF MY FEET."

In the Disney film, *Frozen,* young Anna falls blindly in love with Hans. Their instant, unmistakable chemistry leads Hans to propose to Anna post-duet. And she eagerly says yes, because why not? They're so close, they're already finishing each other's sandwiches... It's ideal.

But is it really ideal? So many single people blow off potential partners based on this momentary lack of intense emotion. In other words, they're drinking the Disney Kool-Aid.

Take Lindsey for example. After a date with Rick, she didn't see stars or experience uncontrollable chemistry with him. She thought, "Oh well, he was nice, but he obviously isn't a good fit for me." (Take note of the use of the word "obviously." This is how deeply we have been programed to believe this fairy tale!)

Even though Rick was interested in her, had a great career, a great family, and a kind heart, and asked her out on a second date, she NEVER saw him again.

Like so many single people, she felt this pressure, as if she needed to know whether he was her future husband after the first date.

Because he didn't sweep her off her feet, and she still felt the need for closure, she sent him a message that said, "You're a great guy. We're not a great fit. I wish you luck!"

Instead of taking the time to get to know Rick, in the same way that she would get to know a new friend, Lindsey chose to never see him again because she didn't have this, extraordinary, magical, Disney experience.

And because she didn't go out on this second date, *she missed a potential opportunity to build something great with a quality person.*

Other relationships take time, such as a new friendship, a relationship with a coworker, a neighbor, etc. We never expect to just know any of them instantly or make some huge long-term commitment. Why should it be any different with someone we might marry?

LOVE AT FIRST SIGHT IS THE EXCEPTION, NOT THE RULE.

Movies in Hollywood like *Shakespeare in Love and Moulin Rouge* will back up this limiting belief that, "You should just know someone is 'The One' for you on the first meeting." How irrational is that?

Lindsey had no idea that she didn't need to make any decision after this date. She didn't know that she could just enjoy it for what it was, stay open to what could unfold, and see if he even pursued her. Instead, she frantically pulled out her phone and made the best judgement call she could because she was so invested in believing this fairy tale as the truth.

Listen up! You're never going to know if a man will be your future husband on your first date. You won't even know if he's going to be your future husband after date two, date five, or even date ten. It takes time to get to know someone.

"LUST AT FIRST SIGHT" IS PREVALENT AND REGULARLY CONFUSED FOR LOVE

Many people mistake "level 10" attraction with love at first sight.

I find that chemistry and attraction are overvalued when single people are in the process of choosing a long-term potential partner. I'm not saying you shouldn't have chemistry. I'm not even saying chemistry is a bad thing, but if you're serious about finding a quality person, you need to start basing your dating decisions on reality. Start looking for the qualities in a person that would make a good long-term partner, rather than worrying so much about the sparks. Good chemistry alone does not a good partner make.

You know those moments where your body instantly reacts to the mere sight of someone? Those are your hormones gearing up for a sexual romp, not the beginning of a lifelong, loving marriage.

This fairy tale can absolutely get in the way of you finding someone who would be a great fit for you and your life in the long run. That's why I warn each of my clients of this tricky pattern early into our work together.

Choosing a partner based purely on the amount of chemistry you have with someone is a HUGE problem in our dating culture today. Do you know how many single people miss out on a potentially wonderful relationship because of this fairy tale? It's brutal. And then they wonder why they're still single.

> *First and foremost, for me, is CHEMISTRY. If it's not fireworks and Moulin Rouge, then there's nothing for me. - Frances, a research participant*

Love at first sight is a rare occurrence. It's the exception and should NOT be considered the rule. *Frozen* actually turns love at first sight into a regrettable mistake, by having Anna become instantly smitten with Hans — accepting his proposal without question and later, going as far as to actually rely on him to save her life — only to discover he's a liar with ulterior motives.

THE DARK SIDE OF BEING SWEPT OFF YOUR FEET

Just like Hans lifted Anna up and led her into a romantic dance, did you know that there are actually men who study the art of seduction? They intentionally manufacture the experience of sweeping a woman off her feet on the first date so they can easily sleep with her. These guys are the pickup artists, or the seduction artists, and they know exactly how to play to this common fantasy. They know how to play the game to get you hooked. They know how to work this fairy tale. They know exactly how to sweep you off your feet and into bed. But these type of men, predatory men, are not interested in a relationship. They just want to have sex and they are using your belief in this fairy tale to make it happen.

> *"You were so desperate for love you were willing to marry me, just like that."*
>
> *- Hans and Anna from Frozen*

If you think you need to be swept off your feet in order to know if someone is right for you, think again. It is not the best criteria to judge whether someone could be a good long-term partner.

Would you rather have a man sweep you off your feet initially, or have a man love and respect you for the rest of your life?

 BREAK THE GLASS SLIPPER FOR "LOVE AT FIRST SIGHT & THE INSTANT CONNECTION."

How do you release yourself of the enchantment of this particular fairy tale fantasy?

There's nothing worse than putting in the effort to date and then writing off each potential candidate because the immediate sparks aren't there.

Allowing love to bloom over time is the only remedy.

Take Susan, for example. She did not "feel it" when she first met Brian. During the first date, she didn't think he was her dream man. She had a nice time, but she didn't "feel that spark" at all. She decided she was not going to see him again. Then, through the coaching, she stayed open to going out on another date with him because he was a good guy, they had a pleasant time, and he was respectful. Add to the fact that he was pursuing her and asking her out on date after date. She accepted his offers to go out on dates because she had fun, felt safe and understood. They even took a trip together! During those few initial months, he became more attractive to her and she started to fall for him.

Fast forward a few years and Susan is married to Brian, even though she was going to stop seeing him after the first date, all because she believed the fairy tale, "I'll know him when I see him."

HOW MANY POTENTIAL QUALITY MEN HAVE YOU MISSED BECAUSE YOU DID NOT "FEEL IT" ON THE FIRST DATE?

Real love blooms naturally over time. People you spend more time with get more attractive as you get to know them. It's natural to fall in love *over time*. Just like the relationship that

Princess Anna develops during her journey with Kristoff.

But if you show up to the date thinking you will "JUST KNOW," you are setting yourself up for major failure in the love department. And you may just miss out on a great guy, maybe one you could end up happily marrying *later*.

Having a magical first date experience is more of a rarity than you think it is, so I encourage people to give their dates a second chance as long as they were respectful, kind, and they had a nice time together.

Dating is the art of getting to know another human being. The first few dates should just be about you enjoying each other's company. That's it. No decisions need to be made.

At the end of *Frozen*, Anna and Kristoff finally get their kiss, but even then, the story leaves off with what feels like the start of a relationship, as opposed to an unrealistic shiny promise of a flawless forever.

******

EXERCISE:

Stay open to the possibility that your man, your guy, your person, may not sweep you off your feet on the first date. He may not sweep you off your feet on the second date, third date, or fourth date.

Practice what I call "fondue dating." It's a term I created to teach women how to slowly get to know a man and to see how he truly shows up for her. When you are making fondue, you need to keep the chocolate on low-heat and continuously stir. The art of fondue making is in the slow burn. If you turn up the heat too high, you will burn the chocolate.

"Fondue dating" is not a fast process. With this style of dating you take time to get to know a human being and see if you have a nice connection. Your "job" is to have fun and to see how it unfolds over time.

After a date ask yourself, "Did I feel safe? Did I feel heard? Did I feel understood? Did we have a pleasant time?"

If so, my advice is to go out on at least 2-3 dates with a guy before you determine whether you want to stop seeing him (unless you felt unsafe and disrespected, of course!). See if he pursues you. Give the connection a shot. It's not so much about giving him a shot, it's about giving the relationship between the two of you a chance to bloom. Beautiful moments are inevitable when time and space is created for connection to happen with a man.

No need to know if he is your future husband. Just have fun and go with the flow. Let go of the fairy tale and embrace the reality that building a true connection takes time.

CHAPTER RECAP:

- Love at first sight is a rare occurrence. It's the exception and should NOT be considered the rule.

- "Lust at first sight" is prevalent and regularly confused for love.

- You're never going to know if a man will be your future husband after your first date. It takes time to get to know someone.

- Choose dating partners based on building a quality connection over time instead of chemistry alone.

- Love blooms naturally over time.

Now you know, choosing a partner based solely on an "instant connection," can lead to many missed opportunities for a long-term, committed relationship. Going forward you can experiment with allowing a relationship to develop over time and in a more natural way. And in doing so, you'll create the possibility for real love.

Now that you freed yourself of this fairy tale, it's time to discover the best type of man for you, and he may not come in the package you expect...

3

Belle's Unexpected Romance with the Beast

"He's Not My Type."

The Enchantress left behind an enchanted rose. If the prince didn't find true love before the last rose petal fell, he would remain a beast forever. Many single women are blinded by their variety of "Prince Charming" and may remain single forever if they stay caught up in believing there's only one kind of guy for them.

In *Beauty and The Beast*, Gaston is every woman's dream in town, all except for Belle, of course. He's tall, dark and handsome. He's got the strong jawline and shoulders. He's confident. No one can eat eggs like Gaston or boast about his own accomplishments like this former military captain can, and every day the single ladies fawn all over him. He seems to fit the "type" that every girl thinks she wants. But is he really that great of a catch?

When I asked over 1000 women what their "type" was, I heard everything from tattooed, athletic, broad shoulders, shaved heads, dark skin with goatees, tall dark, and handsome, nerdy, super smart, and men who wear glasses.

Most people have their own flavor of person they consider their personal "type."

While having a predictable pattern for what you find attractive in someone may be a normal thing in our culture, it's also something that could get in your way of having the love you want.

Where did this concept of having a "type" come from, and why has it become such a standard thing to believe in and base our dating decisions on?

Well… I did a search on QuoDB, an online database of millions of movies and television series and you can use it to find any quote. All quotes are time-based, contextualized, and linked with the IMDB movie database. I typed in the words "not my type" and that quote was found in 2169 films! This is how prevalent this fairy tale is immersed in our minds and constantly affirmed by Hollywood films and TV shows.

Here's a sample of what some of the women specifically said in my research when I asked them, "What is your type?":

- My type is a little geeky and intelligent with a dark sense of humor.
- I dig strong jawlines.
- I definitely gravitate towards darker skin tone, strong facial bone structure, big hands and earnest eyes.
- Intelligent/educated
- 6'2-4", 220 pounds, tattooed, has a job that makes money, preferably entrepreneur, bachelor's degree, never married, no kids, big family that all hang out, social, whiskey and cigar kinda guy, likes to travel.
- Big shoulders, nice hands, nice eyes, nice teeth…
- Dark and handsome!
- Tall, medium build, great smile, successful, ambitious, no young children, athletic...
- Tall, buff lean muscles, light brown skin, goatee or short shaved beard.

- Broad shoulders, nice chest and arms, natural muscular build, gentle eyes, sexy hands, taller than me, curly hair, sweet smile.

What is your "type"?

Many people have a strong preference, but a rare few don't.

A "type" mostly has to do with looks. It rarely has to do with the *qualities* of a person (a focus I teach my clients how to date from).

Take a moment to think about and define the physical traits that you find most attractive and that you find yourself gravitating towards quite regularly.

Sometimes people are unaware that they even have a "type" and say instead, "They're not what I typically like." This is another version of the same fairy tale.

Perhaps you like the professional man in a suit, or the man who has 6 pack abs. Perhaps your type is the silent and nerdy type. Or perhaps you like the cowboy who can Texas Two Step. Some women like the big beefy guys. Most women like tall guys. Some women like artistic types. Some women like men who have long hair. Some women like an edgy man with a shaved head.

Having "a type" is considered a normal thing to talk about and to use as the basis for choosing who we date.

Take Anna for example. A single woman of 42 who loved men with blue eyes. She found them so attractive and only wanted to date men with this eye color. In an attempt to help her see her limited perspective, I asked her, "What if you met a nice gentleman who could really make you happy, would you consider dating a man that had brown eyes or green eyes?"

She said, "No."

I was shocked and could not believe that someone could be so attached to an extraneous preference.

After three years, I recently spoke to this woman again. Guess what? She is still single.

Believing this fairy tale, "He's not my type" has been affirmed into our minds by Hollywood films and has become an accepted part of our culture and lexicon. It's such a normal thing to hear people say, that we don't even blink an eye to it (but you will now).

Closing off all other options and being so attached to "what you typically like" will have a massive impact on your love life.

COOL ARTIST VS NERDY GUY

Take my client Marie for example. She almost missed out on an amazing relationship. Her "type" were guys who looked cool, who had a great sense of style, edgy, and modern. She loved artistic types. She loved this flavor so much, she even married one. He was an extremely talented artist and musician, but over time, the relationship devolved and reached a point where she alone was the breadwinner. She took care of the finances for the family, including supporting their daughter, and she felt frustrated and unsupported. It ended in a painful divorce.

After her breakup, Marie was looking for some support. She hired me to help her get over her past relationship, let go of any pain she was still carrying, and to attract new love into her life. During our sessions, she realized that even though they were together for 8 years, she lost respect for him within the first year of their relationship! However, she ignored this, because in her mind, he was so her "type." She was so attracted to him physically and thought he was so perfect for her. She was in complete denial about the disdain she felt for his life choices, but she still married him because she believed he was for her and she felt like she could make it work.

Once she was healed and ready to date again, she met a nice guy named Sean through mutual friends. He didn't have much fashion sense. He had an average haircut. Some may say that he was even a little dorky because he came from the Information Technology world, but you know what? He was really great to her. He had a great job. He was a nice, stable, and fun person.

Marie resisted Sean at first because he did not fit into the mold of who she could see herself with. He didn't create art. He didn't write music. He wasn't cool and edgy. He was just a regular guy, who was a good father, had a great career and was pursuing her. And more importantly, with him she felt safe, heard and understood.

I encouraged her to stay open to dating him.

Fast forward to today and they are still together. They just bought a house and Marie's daughter and Sean's son get along fabulously.

Imagine if she had stopped seeing him after the first date because he was "not her type?" She may still be single and lonely.

If you're serious about finding a relationship with a quality person and finding your future husband, then you need to be open to people that fall outside of your type.

YOUR "TYPE" HASN'T WORKED OUT SO FAR FOR YOU, SO WHY ARE YOU SO ATTACHED TO IT?

We have been programed to think that we should choose who to date based on our self-created predilections and what we have been conditioned to be attracted to.

It's time to start thinking about *why* you are attracted to a particular image or type of person.

Perhaps your proclivities come from being raised by your stately father, or they are things that are acceptable to your family. Or maybe they come from an idea you formed based off of your first love in high school or being imprinted by the boys you grew up with.

Texas Football Player Boyfriends to Chinese Fiancéé

I recently interviewed a beautiful woman who was a Chinese medicine practitioner in Texas. As a part of her training she studied for many years in China. When she arrived in China, she was single and wanted to experience love. She knew that she was going to be there for a few years, and she didn't want to put her romantic life on hold. She wanted a man and she wanted a man now!

As she put herself out there on the dating scene, she realized that she was not meeting any men that were her "type." She had the experience of not being "attracted" to anyone.

In an effort to shift, she started to look within herself and examine her penchant for certain men. She was raised in Texas and she grew up around football players who were big, strong and tall. She was also raised around Latino men. When she looked closer within herself, she could see that this was her proclivity. Football players and Latino men were most attractive and safe to her because that is who she grew up with. These were the masculine choices she had as a young, blooming woman.

Before she went to China, she would gravitate towards these types of men because they were her favorite. She felt comfortable with them because she was used to them, therefore they were most attractive.

In China, the men not only looked different from the men she typically favored, but they acted different as well.

But she was a woman who was committed to having a connection with a man, so she *consciously shifted* her "type." Even though it felt odd to her at first, she allowed herself to go out on dates with men she would never have been predisposed to go out with in the past.

To find love in China, she dismantled her "type,' and shifted the physical characteristics she found attractive in terms of body type, hair, eyes, looks, and also in terms of the energy men emanated.

She went on many dates during her time there. Before long, she found a great man and they ended up getting engaged!

This woman was able to consciously blow up her own preconceived notions of how a potential partner should look. She faced her own self-created fairy tale head on and opened up her mind to being loved by someone outside of her customary leanings. In other words, she stopped being attached to a "type" and instead, she focused on the *qualities* she really desired in a long-term partner. And the results were nothing short of amazing.

Getting overly attached to your "type" can have detrimental effects on your ability to find true love.

Here's why…

Not only does it stop you from giving that great guy you wrote off after a first date a chance to show up for you… it actually *prevents* you from even getting a first date to begin with! You'll be so quick to shut a guy down if and when he asks you out, simply because he doesn't fit in the mold of what you have been attracted to in the past.

Just imagine how many potentially fulfilling relationships you've missed out on with really great guys, all because you won't go out with men who you have not typically liked in the past.

Sounds pretty crazy when you put it like that, doesn't it?

YOUR "TYPE" IS A FAIRY TALE. IT'S JUST A PERSPECTIVE THAT YOU'VE MADE UP. IT'S NOT REAL.

I see way too many women using this fairy tale to guide one of the most important decisions of their life: who they choose to date to ultimately find their future husband.

You won't even go on a first date to see if this man might be for you because he doesn't look the way that you think he should or he's not who you've dated before, so you just won't even bother.

A connection needs to start somewhere and having a first meeting is where it all begins, but if you refuse to even take the chance and get to know someone because they don't fit the mold of what you typically like, you're shooting yourself in the foot and severely limiting your options for an opportunity for lifelong love.

My husband didn't fit my "type," and thank goodness I was present enough to see the amazing man sitting at dinner with me on our first date. - Amy, research participant

THE NARCISSIST AS A TYPE

While interviewing hundreds of women in research for this book, a common pattern emerged. Many women noticed that their "type" was a narcissist. Instead of noting physical characteristics, they said they fell into the pattern of attracting manipulative and self-centered men. While they didn't want these men to be their "type," they realized these were the type of men they kept choosing over and over again.

Take Frances for example. She said the kind of men she dated were "manipulative narcissists who were tattooed, poor, had no degree, no drive, worked out a lot, were super-hot, and had lots of mental issues." Yikes! And numerous women simply stated that they repeatedly attracted the pathological narcissist.

The women in *Beauty and the Beast* who fell for Gaston because of his handsome ways, failed to look a little deeper to see that he was an egotistical hunter who was determined not to let anyone else win Belle's heart, even if it meant killing her true love.

A narcissist is someone who sees themselves as superior to

everyone around them. Gaston is proud, boorish, uncultured, impolite, narcissistic and misogynistic. He is also arrogant, as evidenced by his setting up a wedding before he even proposed to Belle, under the expectation that she'd approve of becoming his wife.

Gaston's view of women is extremely sexist, even by standards of the time in which the film takes place. And while he appears charming to all of the other women of the village, such as the Bimbettes (who, being products of an upbringing in the village, grew up to see nothing wrong with Gaston's behavior, completely mesmerized by his muscles and handsome face), Belle is the only woman in the entire town who is able to see him for what he really is from the start of the film.

One of my specialties as a dating coach is helping women stop picking the wrong guys and empowering them to see the men they are dating with an expanded view – like Belle.

But as we all know, we don't live in a movie. Your prince charming may or may not look the way you've always imagined him. But the point is, if you stay stuck in your preconceived ideas of what kind of guy he needs to be, if you limit yourself and only open your heart (and your schedule) on rare occasion, you severely limit your chances of finding him.

BREAK THE GLASS SLIPPER FOR
"HE'S NOT MY TYPE."

How do you break out of the bonds of this particular fairy tale fantasy?

Staying rigid in "your type," can keep you single, or in a repeating pattern of misery.

You created your "type," so you have the power to let it go.

Instead of choosing men based on a type, I encourage my clients to not only notice what their type is, so they bring it into conscious view, but to also choose potential dating partners based off of the characteristics that really matter to them in the long run. It's nice to date a hot man, but if he isn't in alignment with what you want for your future, why bother committing?

You are never going to stop being attracted to certain men, period. And there's no reason you should stop! But don't fall into the trap of letting what you typically find attractive be the *only basis* for going out on a date with someone. This limits your options. When you start shutting men down because they're not fitting into your regular category, that's when problems arise. The more you cling to your made-up standard, the more you're going to lower your chances and limit your possibilities at *real love.*

So, what criteria *should* you use to choose dating partners?

When you're ready to let go of your old patterns and finally get different results in dating, I recommend you select dating partners based on what I call your "Dating Compass."

The Dating Compass is a process that's a part of my *Total Partner Clarity Program*. Women who flourish in dating have a definiteness of purpose: they move on their own initiative, and they know where they're going before they start. It's all about gaining clarity on what you want and need in love. Over the course of a few weeks, you discover the qualities your future partner must absolutely have. These top four qualities become the criteria you use to date and identify relationship potential.

When Katie first came to me, she wanted a guy who was funny, handsome, tall, and intelligent. While those are respectable characteristics, everyone wants them! I led her through an introspective journey to get to the heart of the matter — what she truly wanted. You see, she was 38 years old and wanted to get married and have children. Time was ticking. She didn't have time to invest in men that were not in alignment with her heart's desire. When you're dating with the clear intention of finding a partner who is on the same track for marriage and commitment as you, there's a completely different way to date. You actually have to know what you REALLY need and want.

After a few weeks, Katie created her personalized Dating Compass – a man who had integrity, who was loving and protective, and who was emotionally healthy and responsible.

Each time she met a new man, or went out on a date, we would go back to her Dating Compass to see if he fell within this territory. Of course, these characteristics may take a little longer to reveal themselves fully, but she would keep her eye out for men who demonstrated these qualities.

The minute a man did not fall within her Dating Compass, I encouraged her to let him go. For example, when a man she went out with spoke to her about a shady business deal on their first date, we would discuss whether what he revealed through this conversation fell within the characteristic of Integrity (one of her Dating Compass points).

This is how you powerfully sort when you are dating. Dating is a sorting process, and to do it powerfully, you need to know what you truly want. That's why I created the Dating Compass, to simplify the sorting process, and to speed up the time it takes to find a life-long partner who is a great fit for you. (If you are interested in creating your own Dating Compass go to www.cristabeck.com)

After Katie realized that this shady business deal did not exhibit integrity for her, she let that particular man go. If Katie didn't know her Dating Compass (and didn't have me to support her), she would definitely have continued dating this guy because there was so much chemistry and he was her "type" – funny, tall and smart.

It's time to interrupt this fairy tale so you can be open to love in whatever package he may come in. That's what the Dating Compass makes available for you.

> *He's got nice hair... oh, I love his hair. He smells good, doesn't he? He's attractive.*
>
> *He's not my type!*
>
> *Not your type! Okay, maybe not yet. But you meet him, you're nice... and he becomes your type.*
>
> *– from Un monstre à Paris (2011)*

******

EXERCISE:

The first step is to notice what your type is, and if you notice yourself saying, "He's not my type," interrupt yourself.

Be open to new men who fall outside of "your type." When you're single, it's best to stay open to as many possibilities as possible. I encourage you to start accepting dates from men who are outside of your regularly scheduled programming. Just try it.

CHAPTER RECAP

- Most women have their own flavor of man that they consider their personal "type."
- Getting overly attached to your "type" can have a detrimental effect on your ability to find true love.
- We have been programed to think that we should choose whom to date based on our self-created predilections and what we have been conditioned to be attracted to.
- Choose dating partners based on your core values and be open to love in whatever package he may come in.

With your new willingness to release the over attachment to your "type," not only will you get asked on more second dates – you'll get invited on more dates in general. Staying open to men who don't fit in the mold of what you have been attracted to in the past will create more opportunities for true and long-lasting love to enter your life.

It's time now to discover how to rewrite your love story, validate your heart, and be open to a new man who may be right under your nose, however, you may be a little preoccupied...

4

Your Inner Stepmother is Preventing You from Going to the Ball

"I'm Too Busy!"

Just like Cinderella, you too have a wretched Stepmother who orders you around with extra chores, preventing you from meeting your one true love. But Cinderella's tears in the garden bring about a magical evening and open up a portal to meeting her Prince. You have to become your own Fairy Godmother.

As the forced servant in her own household, Cinderella attends to her stepfamily's every beck and call. Even though she's on the job from morning until night and her life's conditions are deplorable, she still tries to keep herself going, by dreaming of a better life someday. Her only friends are a few little birds and mice, whom she sews little clothing for and confides in.

One day, a royal messenger shows up at the chateau with an invitation for all eligible maidens in the Kingdom to come and meet the Prince that evening. Upon hearing the proclamation, Cinderella grows happy that she can also attend, given that it invites "every eligible maiden."

Her Stepmother says she can attend the ball, "if" she can complete all her chores, and "if" she can find something suitable to wear.

The Stepmother spends the rest of the day ordering Cinderella around with extra projects, in an attempt to prevent Cinderella from attending the ball.

In the same way, you have your own "Inner Stepmother" who keeps you busy with work, even though deep down, you want to meet your Prince.

And this "Inner Stepmother" is not just of your own making, it's actually a societal problem. This problem can have negative effects to your health, and it can profoundly affect your love life.

These days it seems like anytime you authentically ask someone how they are doing, no one ever says "fine" anymore. Instead, you get a deep exhalation and the word, "busy." It seems like more and more people these days are scurrying around like the mice in Cinderella who are being chased by Lucifer the cat. You hear everything from "busy" to "crazy busy" to "insanely busy."

And the strangest part of the response is that there is a sense of pride associated with it.

While most people may sympathize with one another by saying, "I can so relate! I am too!" or "I know! I'm crazy swamped right now." or "I need more time to do everything I need to do!"

Personally, I make an effort not to reassure or join the bandwagon.

And here's why:

BEING BUSY IS A FAIRY TALE.

I see people wearing their saturated and overworked schedule like they were just awarded the Medal of Honor by the President of the United States at a formal ceremony in Washington, D.C. Only there's no honor to be had.

And wearing this medal has become a big part of our culture.

There is an agreement that being busy is a good thing.

In the United States especially, you are defined by your

career, and what you produce. Wherever you go, whether it's a networking event, party, or just meeting someone in the street, "what you do" is how you define yourself for strangers.

It's almost as if the subconscious conversation being had is, "I *need* to be busy, or else I am valued less than those people who are producing something."

It's a never-ending cycle.

Especially for single women who want to find love.

I discover different versions of the same fairy tale every day.

I hear:

- "I don't have time to date."
- "I have a very tight schedule."
- "I have a very full life and I don't have room in my schedule to go out."
- "I have a lot of things going on. I have my career and my family and friends. I really just don't have time to meet new men, so I don't."

Just like Cinderella's Stepmother created more work in an effort to prevent Cinderella from going to the ball, you believing this fairy tale keeps you locked up in the high tower away from eligible bachelors.

BEING BUSY IS BECOMING AN EPIDEMIC.

According to the 'Stress in America' survey published by The American Psychological Association, the majority of Americans are aware that they are overstressed, but they also blame being too busy.

It's like being on a merry-go-round that never stops.

Have you noticed that more and more people these days are complaining about being overly tired and not being able to sleep? Numerous people have confided in me through my research that they are on anxiety medication. Recently, a 25-year-old told me she had Acid Reflux. Multiple friends suffer from frequent headaches. Maybe it's my trusting face, but even strangers tell me about their constipation problems or lower back pain. I attribute these ailments to excessive busyness, and so does the medical industry.

According to Dr. Michael Marmot, a British epidemiologist who studies the effects of stress, there are two types of busyness. The most destructive is "busyness without control." This is a type of busyness that affects people who have low incomes. Their economic status does not allow for rest because they need to work two to three jobs just to keep up with all of the bills. Add children to the mix and it can easily become overwhelming, which can lead to health problems caused by this type of stress.

According to Dr. Marmot, the second type of busyness also results in health problems, but it's a malady we bring on ourselves.

What most people don't realize is that the busyness they are experiencing is busyness they CAN control. All of this rushing around and worrying is self-created.

In a quest to understand this obsession with being busy, a team of researchers created a fictional Facebook user, and asked volunteers to look at her posts.

When she posted about working nonstop, people thought she had higher status and more money than if she posted about her leisure time.

And they did the same research in Italy - and the results flipped. People with more leisure time were considered to have higher status than those that were working all of the time.

Now when they published the findings in the Journal of Consumer Research in 2017, one thing was very clear:

BUSYNESS HAS BECOME A STATUS SYMBOL.

How many of you spend more time posting on social media about how busy you are, and perhaps even complaining about it, than you do posting about that awesome vacation you took last year that cost you thousands of dollars? I know you do. Because busyness is honored more than a relaxing vacation. Add to the fact that people DREAD idleness and CRAVE a reason to stay occupied. They even created a term for it called, "Idleness Aversion."

We are uncomfortable with being with ourselves.

In a report in *Science Magazine* called 'The Challenges of the Disengaged Mind' researchers placed people in a room, alone, anywhere from 6-15 minutes. When asked, mostly all of the participants communicated that it was an unpleasant experience to be alone, doing nothing. Here's the interesting thing, when given the choice, nearly half of these people preferred to administer electric shocks to themselves, to be able to get out of the room.

People prefer to hurt themselves rather than feel the discomfort of sitting alone for a few measly minutes.

That's crazy.

What most people don't realize is that the busyness they are experiencing is something they CAN control.

So, what does being busy do for you? We all do it. What does it do for us? It's so prevalent in our culture. It's like the water we swim in. We don't even see it. What are we getting out of it?

I found the answer, and it may be a little uncomfortable to hear.

Busyness isn't just idleness aversion. My theory is that idleness aversion is emotional aversion. That we are TERRIFIED of our feelings. And emotional aversion leads to romantic aversion, a deep reluctance to put yourself on the court and take action in your love life.

WE ARE AFRAID OF OUR FEELINGS.

Most people who are looking for love carry past unresolved hurts. People use "being busy" to avoid their past and current feelings, the discomfort of dating, and the potential of being hurt again.

A generally supported strategy in our culture in dealing with all of the negative and overwhelming feelings after a breakup is to avoid them. Instead of facing them and dealing with them head on, we are highly encouraged by our society to boycott them and to shut them down. We'll get into more detail on what this looks like later in the chapter.

We were not trained how to listen, understand, and care for the depth of our heart with the kind of attention and reverence it needs.

RELATIONSHIPS ARE MATTERS OF THE HEART.

The heart does not work like the mind, like a linear set of logic. Are you ever surprised by the illogical things you say and do, the feelings you can't control, the ways you are affected that you didn't expect? The heart, the emotions of the heart, are deeply affected in any breakup in which you have given yourself emotionally and/or physically (and usually both).

When you were born, your heart was open, and the love and the hurt came without your having much discernment or protection. This level of vulnerability and openness is what allowed these early relationships to be intimate. Any relationship you have as an adult that has some vulnerability and intimacy involves your heart. Often when we go through a breakup, we are left feeling alone, insecure, hurt, angry, obsessed or incomplete and we want it to end. We don't want to feel that way; we want relief, completion, peace, security. Sometimes it feels like too much to bear so we simply shut it out. The problem is, if you shut out the heart and you don't deal with it on its terms — try to use ploys, mental tactics, or fill yourself up with busyness — the heart does not go away. Here's the problem, your hurt heart, with all the unexamined emotions and insecurities swept under the rug, rears its head in all kinds of strange or even harmful ways. You can experience anything from getting physically and emotionally sick, to getting stuck in the pattern of attracting the same type of unhealthy relationship over and over again.

It's time to rewrite your love story – and it all starts with looking at the ways in which you invalidate your heart and emotions.

There are many ways in which we turn away from what we feel. Everyone has their own flavor of avoidance. For example, people deflect by overeating, by watching too much television, drinking heavily and daily, partying, surfing the internet, sleeping around, and by BEING BUSY.

So, you may want to consider, if you're leaning heavily on the fairy tale "I'm too busy," there may be some resentment, sadness, grief, or anger still there. Perhaps there are some old hurts that are still lingering in your space, or fears of being hurt or rejected again.

Could it be that this over-obsession with being busy as a culture is rooted in our inability to be with our feelings?

Let's circle back to that study involving the electric shocks. When I first heard about that study, I was appalled. But then again, it made sense when I thought about the work I do with my clients in the love department. I help people to release the pain from their past relationships and to rewrite their love story, and while most of my clients are ready and willing to do the work to let this baggage go, there are a few that resist. They don't want to confront what they have been sweeping under the rug.

Let's take anger for example. Many people think if they feel their anger, they will potentially get stuck in anger forever. I remember when I was a kid and I would cross my eyes for fun. When my mom saw me do this, she said, "If you keep doing that, your eyes will get stuck that way forever!" Out of fear, I immediately stopped crossing my eyes (until I got older and figured out that my mom just made that up). Similarly, we think if we feel our anger it will get stuck that way forever, but in actuality, the opposite is true. When you allow the anger to come up, it flows through you and gets released.

Instead of being with ourselves and allowing what we feel to flow through us, we do everything we can to side-step it, which includes being busy. We will take on one too many activities, say yes to extra responsibilities at work, and fill our calendar with self-important busyness, just to avoid the horrific possibility of being alone with ourselves. Sadly, we are missing out on the peace and love that resides within.

It's not that you have a "really tight schedule", in reality you have placed your love life on the back burner and have not made it a priority.

Now the question that is begging to be asked is, "Why is your love life not a priority?"

You probably got hurt somewhere along the line. Perhaps it was the last guy, or perhaps it was the one before, but you did what many people do to avoid the painful feelings after a breakup – you got busy. You got so busy, that you got into a habit of being busy.

And saying you are busy gets you off the hook in our society because "being busy" is praised and respected. Therefore, when you say that you're busy, people think, "Ohhhhhhhhh she's busy. She's important. She's needed."

But I'm here to say that "I'm too busy to date" is 100% an excuse. You may be getting mad at me right now for saying this! "But Crista, I am busy! I have my job and I have to work 50-60 hours a week, and then I have my friends and I'm not going to give up my time with my friends. I have my family to take care of. I have to exercise every day. That does not leave time for dating. I'm sorry. It's true. I don't have time to date."

To that I say, "I get it! You have a great career, great friends, great family, great body that you take care of, but I want you to consider that somewhere along the way, you gave up on love. And you've gotten into the habit of being alone."

THERE'S A DIFFERENCE BETWEEN BEING BUSY AND HAVING A FULL LIFE.

You control your life. You control your schedule. You control your priorities, so if having love is important to you, (and I am assuming it is because you're reading this book), you need to let go of this fairy tale and make finding love a priority.

Take Christy, for example. When she came to me, she claimed she was bombarded with work and barely had time to even go to the gym. Just the thought of adding time to meet single men into her intensive schedule was stressful to her.

I told her, "If you're too busy to date, you are going to be too busy to be in a relationship. When you're in a relationship, you need to make time for your partner. You're going to need to make your relationship a priority. Quality time is important. It's time to start making quality time for you, for your love life, and for your future partner, because you don't just want a relationship for a relationship's sake, right? You actually want to have a partnership that lasts. If you're using this excuse now in your present life, you're probably going to keep using this excuse when you're in a relationship, so you really need to interrupt this pattern now."

She was a successful consultant, traveling all around the country, working on different projects. She had a lot of responsibility and traveled 2-3 weeks out of the month for her job.

There was a lot on her plate, but in her heart, she wanted to find a partner and have a family of her own. All of her friends were getting married and she kept wondering, "Why has it happened for them and not for me?" She was 38 years old, time was ticking, and she really wanted kids. However, she kept placing her career and her job as the main priority. She got into the habit of being busy.

For Christy, being on the road that much meant she often wasn't in her own city to date. If she made a connection, she couldn't go out on another date for 2-3 weeks depending on her schedule. Not to mention, this travel schedule was burning her out.

She kept saying she didn't have any time to date, but I did not let her off the hook.

We started to look at the feelings that were underneath the surface and we discovered something important about the first and main pivotal relationship of her life. This relationship had lasted for almost 5 years, and while it was exciting and she felt adored, she also felt an extreme lack of trust with him. He owed her money and he completely forgot her birthday each year, even though his birthday was the day before hers. Kind of hard to forget. But the main issue was that she felt extreme guilt within the relationship because her parents ignored him and didn't want him in her life because he was a different race. Her style of dealing with her boyfriend and her parents was to be nonconfrontational. She sucked everything up and "got over it." She didn't let them know she was upset. She diminished her own needs just to keep the peace, but she was craving safety, security, communication and more presence from her boyfriend.

And from her family, she felt deeply misunderstood, judged for her relationship choice, and traumatized by their family motto: "If we ignore him, he will go away." She experienced so much stress and anxiety because her family did not approve.

After things fell apart with her boyfriend, she never really opened herself up again to another deep, long-term relationship. She had some short-lived boyfriends here and there but nothing stuck. She felt critical about her past relationships. Not to mention feeling tremendous amounts of fear of being judged by her parents again. The immense fear caused her to always second guess herself when it came to men, and from that initial relationship on, she kept her love life hidden from her family.

As a result, she kept busy. She worked hard, climbed the corporate ladder. Went out drinking with her friends and overate a little bit, all in an attempt to not feel what was going on under the surface.

When she began working with me, she didn't know how to feel. She said her emotional side had slowly closed down over the years. She felt like she had to be tough, and not show her cards to any man that came her way.

But soon she discovered that there was still emotional residue in the field between herself and her former partner. She felt deep guilt around the racism that her family projected on to her boyfriend. She felt frustration from him not paying her back thousands of dollars. She had an extreme fear of being judged. These feelings remained unresolved and caused her tension.

But she was ready to do the work.

She started to feel lighter as she felt and released these old and painful memories. She started a new pattern of sharing her feelings. She even had a conversation with her family members about the impact they had on her when they rejected her boyfriend, and how she shut down to men after that.

She started to make herself open to men again. Instead of putting them in the friend zone like she had always done, she chose to be open to men who approached her. Instead of asking herself, "Why is he interested in me?" and being critical of herself, she would say yes when she was asked out. Instead of going up into her head and over analyzing and getting logical, she would smile, play and connect with the men around her.

After she did the work to express and release her feelings and reach a more neutral place, we also had to deal with the logistics of her schedule. I told her we were going to have to shift her work life in order to allow room for love to show up. She needed to start making her personal needs a priority, but she didn't know where to begin.

We looked at her schedule and how we could start to create time for her love life. When we got to the heart of the matter, she confessed that she didn't enjoy her workload or her aggressive travel schedule, but like a hamster on a wheel, she just kept going and going, not taking a moment to tune in with herself to see that she was miserable at her job.

She started to see that she needed to have some serious conversations at work about her workload and what truly worked for her and her life.

The next day, she went into her boss and said, "This amount of traveling doesn't work for me. Being gone 2-3 weeks a month doesn't work for me. I'm getting burnt out and we need to solve this problem. I have some personal commitments I need to take care of in my life and the schedule is just way too off balance for me. Let's talk about how we can make this work."

This was the first step in honoring herself and her needs to feel good in her life. Her boss worked with her and was able to accommodate many of her requests. She was in her hometown more, was given more short-term projects that didn't require a lot of travel, and had some responsibilities taken off her plate.

She then started to create a powerful intention to have a loving relationship – she made this mission a priority and took a stand for herself to have love.

When I asked her what she wanted her dating journey to look like on her way to find her true love, she said, "I want to have the summer to remember. I want to feel free and date lots of men," and that's just what she did.

She began to carve out time in her schedule that was just for dates. She needed to put that time aside so that her calendar reflected her commitment: to find a loving man to marry and create a family with. Getting into action, she scheduled two nights a week on her calendar for potential dates to show up.

I also encouraged her to get her online profile set up and to invest 20 minutes a day to find men online. She could tend her online dating profile from wherever she was and could start making connections with men in her local area, even if she was out of town. After just a few months working together, she was dating like a boss. So many men were interested in her and she was going out on numerous dates.

When we first started working together, her love life was as barren as Cinderella's social circle before the big ball, but now she was in an abundant oasis of men.

Christy's love life was on hold for many years, all because she bought in to the story, "I'm too busy to date" and used it to justify her singleness. She did not make herself and her love life a priority.

If she didn't take the time to interrupt this fairy tale of "I'm too busy to date" she would still be stuck in the stress of traveling so much for her job, worried about being alone, and wondering why all her friends were getting married and not her. But instead, she took responsibility for her love life and took action.

Plus, she got to see that she was not setting boundaries for her own well-being at work and she gained the confidence to request what she really wanted and needed in her life: Time for herself and time to date!

Here's the bottom line: You control your schedule. You control your life. Your life is not outside of your control.

 ## BREAK THE GLASS SLIPPER FOR
"I'M TOO BUSY."

How do you break out of the bonds of this particular fairy tale fantasy?

It's time you let your busyness rest in peace. Trade your busy life for a full one.

A busy life distracts us from what we really care about, and who we really care about. A busy life is all about piling it on, catching up, falling behind, and waking up tired, to do it all over again.

A full life invites us to engage in what we really care about and spend time with the people we really care about. A full life isn't about doing it all but falling asleep at the end of the day content with how you spent your minutes and hours and a pleasant anticipation of the day to come.

A busy life leads to jaw clenching and brow furrowing. A full life encourages you to smile and breathe. The success of a busy life is measured by check marks on a to-do list while the success of a full life is measured by what's on your heart.

Choose a full life.

A busy life seemingly chooses us, but we get to intentionally choose a full life by identifying what matters and getting rid of what doesn't.

A full life allows you to show all the way up for people you love, create the time and space to listen to your heart and soul, and finally connect with what matters most.

******

EXERCISE 1:

For the next 30 days, practice eliminating the word "busy" from your vocabulary. Notice each time you feel pulled to use that word to describe your life.

EXERCISE 2:

Each day, place your hand on your heart, close your eyes, and ask yourself, "What are you feeling?" Notice what answer arises in you. Acknowledge the presence of that feeling.

Now that you know that "being busy" will only distract you from your desire for love, you can begin to explore "feeling your feelings." This new practice and perspective will have you feel open and free, and thereby way more prepared (as well as attractive to amazing men).

Now it's time to see how to find a good man...and yes, they do exist....

5

To Find Your Diamond in The Rough, You Must Leave the Palace

"There are no good men."

Princess Jasmine is not impressed by the overdressed, self-absorbed suitors that her father drags to Agrabah. Forbidden to ever leave, she secretly left her castle alone to break free of the familiar and to explore the new. And what did she find? A whole new world.

Every week I listen to single women tell me how hurt they are, how much they mistrust men, how there's no point to online dating, and how there are no good ones left.

Many women are adamant that they would rather be alone than take a chance on another man, even though they are not satisfied being alone.

Even though the next guy you meet has nothing to do with the last one who hurt you, it's easy to lean on the widespread, accepted fairy tale that there are no good men.

Depending on where and when you type in "All the good men are taken," there are 63,700,000 to 4,410,000,000 results that show up in Google. People are obsessed with this fairy tale that has permeated our society, and many women believe it as the truth.

We even have "studies" completed by Match.com manipulating the numbers to paint a picture that there are no good men.

For example, Match.com ranked Austin, TX men as the worst behaved single men in the country, then they spread this messaging all around the United States. News reporters were reporting it. Facebook ads were running it. Many local new stations, including KVUE in Austin were spreading it via social media. It was EVERYWHERE.

This Match.com Facebook post from KVUE got millions of views. Women were commenting, "See! It's true, there are no good men here in Austin!" Single women were sharing it over and over again, attached with their resigned commentary about their dating experiences. It was spreading like wildfire.

I needed to put a stop to this any way I could. Here again,

society was spreading the same old fairy tale of scarcity.

I contacted the KVUE news station that ran the Facebook ad and they quickly provided me the link to the "research."

It was a collection of responses from a very long survey given to only about 5000 people. It turns out the numbers were not anything substantial.

DISPELLING LAME DATA RESULTS

I immediately sent out this post on social media to combat this fairy tale forest fire:

> *"DO NOT LISTEN TO THIS STUDY" by Match.com that is being spread like wildfire here in Austin!*
>
> *So many people have been reaching out to me to get my thoughts on this.*
>
> *I just reviewed the data of this study after reaching out to KVUE on the validity of this widespread information.*
>
> *The data is shocking. Out of the 5000 singles they gave a survey to, only 383 people were from Texas, and only 80 were from Austin! They are spreading this messaging about Austin based on responses from only 80 people in Austin.*
>
> *ONLY 80 PEOPLE!*

AND, out of the 5000 total people surveyed, only 803 were actually looking for a relationship!

Do you know what that means? If we follow these percentages, only 12 people in Austin who answered this survey were looking for a relationship!

This is such bad info to put out there! It's so discouraging for single women and insulting to single men. It's not correct.

I work hard to dismantle the fairy tales that single people tell themselves that get in the way of taking action to find the love of their life!

Messaging like this just propagates a fairy tale that is NOT true. There are many wonderful men in Austin, TX.

Cultivating a positive environment for my single ladies to thrive in their dating life is my mission. When I hear something like this Match.com study, I want to shout from the rooftops, "Don't believe this sweetheart! It's not true."

And when you believe this fairy tale, that "there are no good men" as "the truth," it weighs on your psyche. It leads women to think, "Why bother dating if there are no good men out there?" If you allow this line of thinking to permeate your thoughts, it can leave you feeling resigned and perhaps even a little bitter.

THE IMPACT OF HOLDING ON TO THIS FAIRY TALE

Take Elizabeth for example. When we first met at a party, she told me that she was not meeting any good men. She is a 40-year-old lawyer, with a demanding job, and for the past 10 years she has been single. I immediately wanted to get on a phone call with her to go a little deeper in a private setting. On our call I found out that her last date was 5 years ago. She had negative feelings towards men thinking, "Why waste my time? Guys are just going to hurt me anyway." And because of this line of thinking she unconsciously closed off the possibility of having the connection and partnership she truly wanted.

And when we looked some more, she was able to see that she never goes anywhere to meet new single men and was not investing any time in this area of her life. She was cute, smart, successful and if she would have only put herself out there to meet new men, I know for a fact she would have met someone.

The sad part of this story is that Elizabeth was not willing or open to do the work to adjust her perspective, and because of this I could not help her. She was just not interested in changing this part of her life, even though deep down she wanted someone to go on adventures and share life with. But in the end, she preferred to hold onto the story "There are no good men."

There are many reasons why people want to hold onto this fairy tale. Perhaps you have been hurt by men in the past, or you haven't met anyone recently who has knocked your socks off, or maybe you were raised by an unkind father.

Now Elizabeth is an extreme case of someone believing the fairy tale, but where are you on the spectrum? Are you willing to let go and be open to the fact that good single men exist?

If you find yourself thinking they don't exist, or you agree with the "no good men" perspective, I invite you to spend a little time reflecting on what experiences in your life have helped feed this story and made you believe this.

Because from my professional experience, there are lots of good men.

Take Josh, for example. An influencer and podcast host committed to wellness. He's single and he's looking for a long-term partner.

Take Brian, an entrepreneur who works out daily, has two delightful kids, empowers his community, and has a beautiful home. He's single and looking for a lifelong partnership.

Or Marc, a retired Air Force veteran, who now works in the tech industry, who travels the world, skis, and does triathlons.

He's looking for his future wife.

These are all good men. You know how I know? Because I have personally spoken to each one of them. I speak to single men all of the time who are 100% committed to doing what it will take to find the love of their life. These are good, solid men. I'm here to tell you that they are out there ladies, you just need to expand the bubble you have been living in.

Just because you have had experiences with some bad apples, doesn't mean that they are all bad!

GO TO THE WRONG PLACES, YOU WILL MEET THE WRONG GUYS

I was talking to a woman recently and she said, "There are just no good guys. I'm not meeting anyone, just a lot of slime balls. I'm so frustrated."

I got curious about this experience she was having. I thought, how was she attracting all these men that weren't great men? Where was she spending her time? What was going on?

I asked her, "Where are you meeting these men?"

She said, "I go out to bars and clubs really late at night. They're all jerks!"

So, I asked her, "Is there any place else you go, or anything else you do, that has you meet new single men?"

And she said, "No, just the club."

So here she is going out dancing at night, drinking with her friends, and then she meets all these guys at midnight or one in the morning. They are predominantly men who are drinking and hoping to score that night. You rarely hear straight men say, "I just gotta dance tonight. Forget the girls. I just gotta dance."

So, I told her, "Here's the problem. You're putting yourself in an inebriated and low-vibe environment which is attracting this type of man. I'm not saying all men that go out to bars late at night are bad guys, but these men are drunk and many of them are looking for one thing: To find someone to have sex with them. That is their main intention, so they position themselves around other drunk women so they can achieve their goal. If a man has the intention of doing that, is he the kind of guy you are looking for? You may want to consider that the environments you're in may have to do with why you are meeting certain types of men."

And it is worth considering that a "good man" may behave differently towards you because of how YOU show up in a certain environment and what they may perceive you are wanting.

WHERE ARE ALL THE GOOD MEN?

I hear this question often, but the question that women should be asking is:

Who is the best type of man for me and where is THIS type of man located?

Saying you want a good man is so vague. As I explained earlier in this book, I guide my clients through the process of building their own Dating Compass so they can know exactly the kind of man they're looking for. Then they can strategically place themselves in the locations where this type of man may be.

Take Soumya for example. She wanted a relationship built on a solid foundation of peace and love. She wanted a stable family life filled with healthy food, lots of fun and quality time together.

After doing the Dating Compass process she discovered that in order to fulfill this experience she wanted in a relationship, she needed a man who was kind, family oriented, generous, and financially stable.

These were the qualities she was looking for in a partner. These characteristics were her Dating Compass, which she used to guide her towards the right man for her.

From there, we were able to think about potential locations where this type of man would be. As we brainstormed, we came up with some great ideas: professional networking events, book signings, personal development seminars, single parent meet-ups, and professional organizations. These locations naturally arose from her being in tune with her Dating Compass.

ALL THE GOOD MEN _YOU KNOW_ ARE TAKEN.

The key words here are: you know.

To take your love life to the next level, it's all about meeting the good men that you have not met yet. It's time to expand your network and meet new single guys, outside of the places you typically frequent. It's time to expand your sphere.

Princess Jasmine from Aladdin was tired of the same old superficial and self-absorbed suitors that her father kept bringing to the palace. Because of her status as the princess of Agrabah, unluckily, Jasmine was forbidden to ever leave the castle walls, spending her life sheltered within the confines of the royal home. Despite living a lavish life, Jasmine often felt suffocated by the laws of her kingdom, which restricted her from socializing with her subjects. These restrictions ultimately prevented Jasmine from making any connections, or making any real friends, aside from Rajah.

In some ways, you are like Princess Jasmine, staying within the confines of the palace of your own making. You stay within the familiar walls of your home, family, work and friends –or even the safety behind the screen of your dating app.

How did Jasmine meet Aladdin? She secretly left the palace alone.

And while you have probably guessed by now that I wouldn't be a fan of Aladdin and Jasmine meeting, falling in love, and getting married in 3 days, I do fancy Princess Jasmine's tenacity.

GOING OUT ALONE IS LIBERATING

Take Stephanie, for example. I spoke some uncomfortable truths to her when she was in a dark place wrestling with her single motherhood and the terrifying prospect of dating again after a long, celibate sabbatical.

One of those truths being that she just needs to get out there…. anywhere. Here she was, this beautiful woman who just got in a rut of being a single stay at home mommy. One of the challenges I gave to her was to get dressed up and feel pretty, go to a luxurious hotel bar, and sit there alone with a fashion magazine – and be open to talk to men.

This was so scary for her, but she did it! She stepped out of her "palace" just like Jasmine. The first time no men spoke to her, but the next time she started to meet new men. She did that faithfully every other weekend for 6 months, which helped her to gain confidence and genuine appreciation for herself. Going out alone to the bar wasn't about picking up men, it was about her facing her fear of going out alone and learning how to date herself first. And of course, many men approached her, and she went out on dates.

She became super selective; and even began to value herself so much that she honestly wondered if she'd ever find anybody worthy of her and her son's life.

But she now has an incredible partner and she writes to me often about him. She didn't meet him at that fancy hotel bar, but that experience opened up her confidence and heart so when she met her man just 4 months later… boy was she ready.

We metaphorically forbid ourselves to leave our castle walls…. but going out alone can be a liberating experience.

 **BREAK THE GLASS SLIPPER FOR**
"THERE ARE NO GOOD MEN."

How do you break out of the bonds of this particular fairy tale fantasy?

Leaving your palace is the only antidote.

There are opportunities to meet good, single men everywhere. You need to get yourself out there in the world, with your eyes wide open and with a willingness to go to new places and try new things. One of the first exercises I have my clients do is to simply make eye contact and smile with at least one new man a day. Then we move into making eye contact and smiling to multiple men a day. It all starts with being open and receptive to men.

The next step is to know what you are specifically looking for in a man and for your future.

And then finally, placing yourself in new locations where this type of man may be.

Below are some ideas and strategies, as well as places where a lot of single men gather and activities in which men participate.

But remember, the first step is getting clear on your Dating Compass and what you're looking for so you can be targeting the right places and right type of men for you. Ready to learn how to rub shoulders with the world's most eligible bachelors, and have them all to yourself? Let's start with attraction.

HOW TO BE THE MOST ATTRACTIVE WOMAN IN THE ROOM

She isn't the prettiest, the most in shape, or the funniest. People may say that the most attractive woman in the room is the woman who holds her own in conversation. A woman who has a confident and flirtatious laugh. Or knows what men think and desire.

Yes, all of these things make a woman attractive. But take a look around you the next time you are at a networking event, finance seminar, or even an electronics store.

Who is the most attractive woman in the room?

She is the woman who is the ONLY woman in the room.

The best places to meet men are the places where the ratio of men to women is much higher. If you don't go out a lot or you often complain that you don't meet many men, you definitely need to place yourself where the men are overflowing and position yourself as the only woman in the room.

Here are locations where there is an excess of men:

- Seminars: investment, finance, business, real estate.
- Tastings: scotch, whiskey, wine, cigars.
- Shows: classic cars, boats.
- Stores: high-end men's department, electronic/computer, golf stores.

If you want to meet men organically, you need to do what men do. Go to places that are centered around male-dominated activities:

- Classes: Martial arts, rock climbing, boxing
- Clubs: golf, sailing, scuba diving, poker.
- Sports events: basketball, hockey, football, golf.

Every new location you frequent will deepen your dating intelligence. You'll discover for yourself what it's like to be the center of a lot of men's attention. You'll have plenty of men to choose from and you will no longer be complaining that you don't meet any new men!

The world's most eligible bachelors are right within your reach, you just have to be brave enough to go to these places you may have never been before.

Can this list help you interact with more men on a more regular basis?

You bet it can.

Will this list expand the amount of dates you get asked on?

Absolutely.

With this list of locations, you have the opportunity to step into a world where you will be surrounded by quality men, dates, and the possibility of love.

Make a decision you won't regret. Get out of your palace and meet your guy.

******

EXERCISE:

Be Princess Jasmine this week and leave your castle. Get out there. Perhaps you can pick one of the locations mentioned in this chapter. Go on. See what it is like to go alone or bring a girlfriend to an environment filled with men. Notice which people approach you. Notice how you feel inside.

CHAPTER RECAP

- Just because you have had experiences with some bad apples, doesn't mean they are all bad!
- To take your love life to the next level, it's all about meeting new men that are outside of your familiar sphere.
- Going out alone is transformational and liberating. Try it.
- The most attractive woman in the room is the one who is the ONLY woman in the room.

Now that you know that believing that there are no good men will only leave you feeling lonely and bitter, stepping out of your comfort zone will have you facing your fear of going out alone. You're learning how to date yourself first so when the right guy comes along, you will know exactly what you like.

Next we'll dive into the number one thing men are attracted to… a secret power a woman can possess at any stage of life…

6

Add A Little Bit of Pixie Dust and You Can Find Love at Any Age

"I'm too old to date."

Peter Pan is the boy who never wanted to grow up. He preferred to live in a world full of adventures and magic. He kept that spark within and never let go of his wildest dreams. But many people lose that childlike inner sparkle they had when they were younger, and there comes a time when you have to clap harder for your inner Tinkerbell.

If we choose to, we can learn from anything and anyone. Even Peter Pan can be a wise teacher if we open ourselves to the meaning of his story.

Peter Pan is a story of how we lose imagination and freedom as we grow up.

> *"No matter how hard we try to be mature, we will always be a kid when we all get hurt and cry."*
>
> *- J.M. Barrie, Peter Pan*

Don't try to grow up too quickly... or at all. Keep that inner child alive.

When it comes to being single and on the dating scene, many people have lost the spark so much so that they doubt that they can find love – based only on the amount of years they have been on this earth. I hear women say:

"Men only want to date younger women."

"I'm too old to date."

"I'm too old to find love."

"I have limited choices."

You'd be surprised by the age of the women who are actually saying this!

You'd think they'd be in their seventies or eighties or something like that. But no, it's often women in their thirties and forties who are saying they're too old!

Where does this pressure come from to be young in order to be able to find love?

Hollywood. I don't think I need to convince you of this one.

Turns out, the pressure to look young doesn't stop even when you've reached iconic status. The legendary actress, Carrie Fisher, said she was pressured to lose over 35 lbs. to reprise her role as Princess Leia in *Star Wars: The Force Awakens* when she was 58 years old. She was pressured to lose weight in an effort to make her look younger, like her younger Princess Leia self.

"They don't want to hire all of me – only about three-quarters!" she said.

"Nothing changes. It's an appearance-driven thing. I'm in a business where the only thing that matters is weight and appearance. That is so messed up. They might as well say 'get younger,' because that's how easy it is."

If you're saying "I'm too old" to yourself (and to others), realize this is yet another fairy tale that has been instilled in you. The message is clear from Hollywood: In order to have what you want in life, you need to be young and fresh. We have been brainwashed to think this. It's been fully integrated into our thought process and we believe this fairy tale as the truth. We don't see it as a limiting belief. We relate to it as if it is THE

TRUTH.

If you couldn't tell by now, I'm obsessed with typing phrases into Google to see how many results there are that talk about specific topics. I typed "too old to date' into Google. There were about 21,500,000 results!

And you know how Google will suggest similar searches?

Here are some of them:

"When are you too old to date?"

"I'm 58. Am I too old to date?"

"Am I too old for online dating?"

People are obsessed with wondering whether they're too old to date.

Where did this obsession/perspective come from?

Here's how Hollywood has made women believe they are too old to find love:

The commonplace practice of casting a much younger female against a much older male has been prevalent since Hollywood's golden age:

Audrey Hepburn was 25 and Humphrey Bogart was 55 in the 1954 movie, *Sabrina*.

Kim Novak was half the 50-year-old James Stewart's age during filming of 1958's *Vertigo*.

Recently Maggie Gyllenhaal, at age 37 was told she was 'too old' for a role opposite a 55-year-old male actor.

"There are things that are really disappointing about being an actress in Hollywood that surprise me all the time," she said. "I'm 37 and I was told recently I was too old to play the lover of a man who was 55. It was astonishing to me. It made me feel bad, and then it made me feel angry, and then it made me laugh."

Hollywood finds itself under increased scrutiny for its failure to represent women fairly on screen when it comes to age. And this failure to represent women fairly has had an impact on what we think is possible in our love lives. If we saw women of all ages being celebrated and represented on screen, if we saw women in their 30's, 40's, 50's, and 60's having thriving dating lives and love lives, would we believe that we were too old?

The Bond movie, *Spectre*, won praise for casting 50-year-old Monica Bellucci opposite 47-year-old Daniel Craig. And you know why they cast her – because no matter what age that woman gets, she has this amazingly sexy presence that oozes from the screen, AAAAANNNNNNND, it was Hollywood's way to try to represent women fairly. But the movie's other two "Bond girls", Léa Seydoux and Stephanie Sigman, were both in their late 20s, and the long-running spy saga has also made a habit of pitching 007 against love interests half his age. Roger Moore, then 57, romanced 29-year-old Tanya Roberts in the Englishman's final outing as Bond, 1985's *A View to a Kill*.

"I'm too old" is a fairy tale that has been propagated by Hollywood to the detriment of our own love lives.

In the QuoDB, the online database which stores all of Hollywood's screenplays for film and TV, I typed in "she's too old" and that line alone was found in 227 stories. When I typed in "too old" the results were 5,555 titles. This prevalence came as a surprise, even to me. Hollywood is ramming the message that we are too old down our throats! So, it's not your fault that you have believed this messaging.

Believing you're too old is a story, but it mainly functions as a block.

It's blocking you from having the experience you want. You get to choose what you want to believe up there in your brain, but if you're going to believe "I'm too old," then you will be too old. As you think, so you become.

MEN ONLY WANT YOUNGER WOMEN = FALSE.

According to Alison Armstrong, (one of my relationship heroes), men are attracted to a woman's aliveness, confidence, and femininity. Younger women tend to exude this, which erroneously has women thinking that men want younger women. In reality of course, this energy can be present in older women too! But often, women end up shutting down this alive, vivacious, youthful side of themselves.

This is usually due to relationship failures, which cause them to grow bitter and spend their lives ignoring the things that make them feel alive. When they show up on a date, they might come off as guarded, righteous, and depleted. Then when they don't get asked on a second date, they immediately think it has to do with their age. But in reality, it's HOW they are showing up to the date. I know plenty of women who are in their 30's, 40's, 50's, and above who are being hit on by men in their 20's! It's all in what you are exuding that attracts men, not an age.

How many men do you hear that are hot for Helen Mirren? A lot! And the actress is 73 years old at the writing of this book. 73! And she is still turning heads and makes men swoon. Why? Because she exudes that sexy confidence and soft femininity that drives men wild.

I spend a lot of time on the phone with single men for my business and research purposes. They tell me all kinds of things they're looking for in a partner, but basically, they want a woman that they feel good around. They want a woman that's happy and vibrant. They want a woman who cares about herself and has confidence. They want a woman they can build a life with. Someone who's successful and has something going for her life. These are men in their 30's, 40's, and 50's. And you know what they rarely ever say?... That they want a younger woman.

That's why I teach my female clients who want to attract a man to get in tune with their femininity, to feel alive, and get inspired by life no matter what age they are.

Sometimes I find that when women get older, they don't keep up with their life force, energy, and femininity. Many women overwork and stop taking care of all parts of themselves – mental, emotional, and spiritual. Some women are just not showing up that same way they showed up when they were younger.

"All you need is faith, trust and a little bit of pixie dust."

We tend to take life too seriously, and to forget that magic does exist within each of us. To find it, we need to believe.

YOU CAN FIND LOVE AT ANY AGE

We all know the woman in her 60's who put herself out there and snagged that great man.

We've all seen those videos on Facebook where the cute 90-year-olds that met in their group home get married. They didn't say "I'm too old." They were just two people who wanted to be in a relationship, they found one another, and then they got married.

I'll make a bet that you personally know people who are older than you who are single and dating.

But this dang fairy tale is sabotaging your love life.

Have you met anyone that got married in their sixties, seventies, eighties, nineties? I have. This is the truth. Believing this made up story is a perspective and it's one that's going to shape how you see everything: dating life, love life, and even yourself... if you let it.

It leads you to not put yourself out there. You feel like there's something wrong with you because of the number of years you've been on this planet. Your age has nothing to do with your ability to find love. Your mindset has to do with your ability to find love.

Take Kathy, a 44-year-old woman and single mom of two teenagers who asked in our first conversation, "Can I find a relationship at my age?" She had a great career as an accountant and a nice house. She believed that love might not happen for her and she wasn't sure how to find it, which is why she reached out to me. She felt lonely, missed the physical component of having a relationship, and was really bummed out.

Because of her "age," she felt like she had fewer opportunities to find a man and she didn't know how to look for him.

She deeply wanted a relationship and to get married again and she thought that the reason she was not having success with finding love was because she was "over the hill." Because this fairy tale is so prevalent, she immediately grasped on to it to make sense of the experience she was having.

With Kathy, the problem wasn't a random statistic about how many years she had been alive – Kathy's picker was broken. She didn't know how to sort men. She didn't know how to recognize whether a man was good for her or not. She just kept spending time with men who were not serious about a relationship.

So, after working together, she built her Dating Compass and got clear on what she wanted – a loyal, attentive, respectful and emotionally mature man. This clarity helped her believe again. It strengthened her confidence because now she knew specifically what to sort for. She realized that she was letting her age cause her doubts, but the truth of it was that she did not trust herself to choose correctly. Having that hope again infused her with radiance and a youthful spirit.

After she put herself online, plenty of men her age, younger, and older wanted to date her.

Then after 3 months she went exclusive with a man who was in alignment with her. He would send her sweet texts. He sincerely loved spending time with her. He would take her out on fun dates. And if she hadn't interrupted this fairy tale, she might still be single and blaming her age.

Peter Pan told Wendy that she needed happy thoughts in order to be able to fly.

> *"Just think of happy things and your heart will fly on wings forever in Never Never Land."*

That's all it takes. Just know that whatever age you are – it's the best age you can be.

 **BREAK THE GLASS SLIPPER FOR**
"I'M TOO OLD."

How do you break out of the bonds of this particular fairy tale fantasy?

Sprinkling a little pixie dust on your life and unleashing your inner child will do the trick.

In Peter Pan, Pixie Dust is a magical golden glitter-like powder that grants the abilities of flight. What kind of pixie dust can you start to shower over your life that would bring out your magical inner child?

Instead of thinking you're "too old," how about you start focusing on *activities that make your inner child happy?*

It's time to stop taking everything so seriously. We devote so much of our time and attention on work, responsibilities, and carrying the weight of the world that we leave little room to play and nourish our own needs. We constantly worry and obsess about the future. We beat ourselves up when things don't go perfectly smooth.

Being an adult can be tough. Once we start "adulting" in life, by paying for college, buying the house, paying the bills, and forging into "real life," it can be difficult to release ourselves at times from the expectations, the pressures, and the need to always be responsible.

During this transition to adulthood, sometimes we lock that child within us down in the basement of our soul. We forget to dream, believe in miracles, and live in full enthusiasm and freedom.

Do you even remember what it's like to run barefoot in the grass, to giggle at the sight of two squirrels chasing each other, or sing in the bathtub?

There's some expectation that once you have "grown up", all things child-like need to go away. What we haven't realized is that a lot of the vitality and natural enthusiasm we had as children were our most attractive qualities and we can channel that life force at any stage of life.

******

EXERCISE:

Discover what your personal pixie dust is – the activities that awaken joy and enthusiasm.

Take a little break from adulthood every day and find the simple pleasures in what it's like to be a kid again.

Here are some ways I personally keep young, vibrant, and playful!

Shake your booty. This is my personal favorite. I love dancing my heart out. Do you ever watch a child dance? They are free and truly feel the music. Go ahead, turn up that music and dance like nobody's watching… (so what if the neighbor sees, perhaps you'll inspire them too).

Skip. Seriously, skip. Once a day, skip to the bathroom, or down the sidewalk, or over to your car in the parking lot. Who cares if someone sees? I promise you'll feel a lot lighter afterwards.

Clap your hands. I clap when I reach a goal, or when a friend reaches a milestone. I clap to celebrate anything and all things. Getting enthusiastic about the small things brings joy to the simple things in life. To be enthusiastic, you must act enthusiastic.

I encourage you to add these three things to your everyday existence or come up with your own. Perhaps asking a lot of crazy questions, giving big hugs, giggling with girlfriends, or dreaming beyond your wildest dreams awakens your inner child.

Whatever you choose to integrate, these actions will create a new perspective to keep things on the lighter side of life and cultivate a more optimistic and happier view of ourselves, life, and romance.

At last you can free yourself from the painful story you've created around your age… The only antidote is letting your inner child shine and allowing this to create a magical connection.

Now you're ready to see how to bring your feminine energy alive in a way that will captivate the right man and make him feel so good he wants to stay…

7

Only True Love's Kiss Will Save You from Your Own Reflection

"I'm not attractive enough."

Princess Fiona hid away from sight after the sun went down for fear that she was ugly. "This is not how princesses are supposed to look." Little did she know that love was right around the corner for her despite believing she could only be loved if she looked a certain way.

Princess Fiona, from the movie *Shrek*, is locked in a dragon-guarded castle awaiting a knight to rescue her. Only a kiss from her true love can break the curse that haunts her at night. But when her saviors finally arrive, they aren't what she expects. A sweet-talking donkey and an irreverent ogre named Shrek, whom she mistakes for a knight, sweep in.

Safely away from the dragon, Fiona demands that Shrek

remove his helmet and kiss her. He removes his helmet, and she is shocked and disappointed to find that he is an ogre. Shrek tells her he is only delivering her to Lord Farquaad, who will marry her.

We soon discover Fiona's secret curse – at night, she herself turns into an ogre. She says each night she turns into "this, this horrible, ugly beast" and she was placed in a tower to await the day her true love would rescue her.

"I'm a princess, and this is not how a princess should look!" she exclaims. And this is the reason she needs to marry Farquaad tomorrow before the sun sets... because only her true love's first kiss can break the spell.

You are like Princess Fiona and think there's a certain way you're supposed to look.

You ask: "Mirror, mirror, on the wall, who's the fairest of them all?"

And the mirror responds,

"Not you. You are not the fairest. You are not the most attractive. You are not the prettiest."

Heart sinks

Would you keep a mirror around that actually said that to you?

No. Of course not!

But you do listen to this mirror and you believe what it tells you. This mirror is the voice in your head that constantly tells you that you are not attractive enough.

And you eat it up!

You listen. You believe. You don't even question it!

And because you BELIEVE that you're not attractive enough, why bother even trying to find love?

From childhood we are taught to compare ourselves to others. We are taught in movies and television that there is a standard of beauty and we absolutely need to measure up!

Our hot pursuit of beauty is influenced by global media and celebrity culture.

Whether your exposure to celebrities is through television, movies, or tabloid covers in supermarket checkout lines – the barrage of the enhanced and heavily edited 'ideal' is undeniable. Just look at the fashion, cosmetics and diet industries and their influence on what we view as attractive. You either have "it" or you don't.

This concern for being attractive enough is an obsession.

In a recent survey, 68% of girls thought they were not pretty enough and a startling one in four would change everything about herself physically, if given the chance.

When I am on the phone with potential clients, I hear anything from "I'm not pretty enough" to "I'm not beautiful enough to date."

They believe that because they don't think they meet society's standards for beauty, that is the reason they're not finding a relationship. But if you've been paying attention in previous chapters, I bet you can guess the real reason they aren't getting results…. they aren't taking action and putting themselves out there! But for some reason, they initially think it has to do with their level of attractiveness above all else.

I'm here to say that this is bogus.

"Attractive enough" doesn't exist, because no one gets to decide what pretty is as a standard.

Of course, we can all agree that if you look like a movie star, more men are going to stare at you when you walk through the grocery store. But just having guys stare at you doesn't actually get you into a happy, loving relationship!

Do you know how many women I've met and spoken with over the years who fit the societal standards of "beautiful" to a T, and yet still can't seem to find a loving partnership? The answer is A LOT. Enough to know that it takes more than that to find love.

Because although fitting society's beauty standards may help you get attention from men, it won't help you form a real connection. It won't help you attract the right kind of man. And ironically, it won't even help all that much with feeling confident and self-assured on dates. The fact is, no matter what we look like, we all have our insecurities.

But as a heavy media consuming culture, we've become convinced that pretty only looks one way and if you don't have it, too bad for you.

What are the consequences of this? When you look at yourself in the mirror and you see that you don't fit the standard, eventually you sigh, and give up. "I'm not beautiful," you think. "I don't look right."

Believing this fairy tale keeps you in the dragon-guarded castle of your own making.

This is not your fault. This fairy tale has us all screwed up in the head.

And what has believing this fairy tale done for your life? What does this fairy tale prevent you from experiencing?

Take Sue, for example. A 42-year-old virgin who thought she wasn't a classic beauty. (I actually hear that one a lot too, "I'm not a classic beauty.") When she came to me, she hadn't been on a date in several years. She'd never had a boyfriend. She was tired of being single and wanted to do whatever she could do to shift this pattern of being single. She wanted to get married and have a family, but something was getting in her way – her belief that no one would want her because of how she looked.

She said she felt defeated. She had gotten her hopes up before, but now she was just completely shut down.

As we started working together, there were two things I noticed as her coach:

1. She did not FEEL feminine and alive.
2. She was not taking actions to date and meet men in alignment with the vision of her future.

Through the coaching, Sue started to take actions to feel a sense of vitality and inner and outer beauty. She took belly dancing lessons. She got a makeup makeover. And with each step, she started to exude her own unique blend of attractiveness and aliveness.

We did an online profile makeover with great photos that captured the sunshine part of her personality. We highlighted her penchant for everything 80's, her love of travel, and desire for a God-centered relationship.

Men started reaching out to her!

And then I got this email from Sue:

"BOOM! I gave one of the OKCupid guys my number and said that I'd be available around 9pm and he called at 9:30pm. We just talked for 1 1/2 hours and are going to meet next Tuesday night at adult skate night at 8pm. (After my call with you!)

P.S. He said I was kind of aloof online, but he thinks that I may be a unicorn – a "normal" girl on a dating app…"

Here's this woman, who thought she wasn't pretty enough, who was now starting to experience men pursuing her.

She was elated.

But then a day later I got this email from her:

"GAH!!! Bad development from OKCupid guy …I found out he used to date one of my friends and has anger issues and some domestic violence charges with ALD. And stalked her a little after they broke up. :("

She was definitely bummed because she was getting so close to her first date in YEARS, but with encouragement she kept connecting with men online.

On our next coaching call, she told me that she got on another call with a man and he asked her out for the upcoming Sunday. And he was going to drive 45 minutes to come to take her out to dinner!

Finally, after many, many years, Sue was having her first date with a man!

When Sue first came to me, she felt discouraged and lonely, with a hint of underlying sadness. Being single poked at her feelings of insecurity. She felt out of control. While she was so confident in so many areas of her life, she didn't feel confidence in the area of love because men never pursued her or asked her out. But here she was now, owning her attractiveness, playfully exuding her girly side, and getting her first date! My inner mama bear was proud.

It's so easy to use the fairy tale "I'm not attractive enough" as an excuse as to why you are not finding love. Sue used this story for years to keep her away from feeling the discomfort that dating can bring.

And did you know that this fairy tale affects men as well as women? Well, I don't hear the pretty part, but men do tell me that they think they aren't attractive enough, and they think THIS is the thing that is getting in the way of them having the love they want. But again, it's usually just about them not taking the correct dating actions and not taking some action around feeling handsome. Once these actions start to happen, fun dates start to flow.

There's this whole societal standard of how you're supposed to look. It's a made-up story, but we believe the story. And then we feel bad.

But think about it… Have you ever met anyone who is currently in a relationship who is less attractive than you according to the made-up, societal Scale of Beauty?

Your level of attractiveness has nothing to do with whether you can have a loving partner or not. Seriously, it doesn't.

Comparing yourself to others in this way will sabotage your love life. Believing this fairy tale will stop you from having the experience you really, truly want.

So if you believe you're not the classic beauty, or you are self-conscious about your looks, or you think guys just go by looks, you need to see these thoughts for what they are — ideas you were programmed to believe that are actually false.

Yes, men are attracted to looks, but if you ask most guys why they committed to a woman they will say something like, "I love the way she makes me feel."

Men want to feel good around you.

If you're walking around feeling awesome, feeling attractive, looking and feeling your best, that's attractive.

Guys don't JUST go by looks. Perhaps initially a certain woman will catch their eye, but really, it's the *energy* of how you're carrying yourself. It's the aliveness. It's the confidence, the spunk and the attitude.

If you're basing whether or not you feel attractive on Victoria Secret model standards, you're putting the power in someone else's hands to judge whether you're attractive or not. You're letting it affect your confidence and self-worth, all for no good reason. Take that power back!

It's time to claim your own attractiveness.

It's time to claim your own worthiness.

It's time to claim it for yourself.

Your guy **is going to adore you just the way you are.**

BREAK THE GLASS SLIPPER FOR
"I'M NOT ATTRACTIVE ENOUGH."

How do you break out of the bonds of this particular fairy tale fantasy?

Only love's first kiss can break the spell. But love's first kiss is not what you may think it is.

We see over and over again in Disney movies the princesses that need that "act of love" to be freed from the spell. Sleeping Beauty, Snow White, Ariel from The Little Mermaid, Beast from Beauty and the Beast and Fiona from Shrek are all in the same boat.

But in this day and age in your pursuit to find love, it's not a magic kiss from a man that you need to find your one true love. It's all about giving YOURSELF Love's True Kiss. Deeply loving yourself will break the spell of feeling unattractive.

Only you know what actions you need to take to truly love yourself and to feel attractive from the inside out. It's about being deeply in tune with you and what makes you feel alive.

It's time to fully claim your own attractiveness.

How does one start to claim their own attractiveness? Let's start in a light and playful way.

Recently I was on a coaching call with a bunch of single ladies and we were discussing the actions they could take to actually feel more attractive and feel good.

The women had a variety of answers:

Daily meditation

Going for walks in nature

Getting my hair blown out

Getting a makeup makeover

Stop going out to the supermarket with my curlers in

Kickboxing class

Clearing out the clothes in my closet that I don't feel good in

Wash my hair

Personally, I dislike washing my hair. Washing my hair and blowing it out takes a long time because my hair is long and thick. Confession: Sometimes I go 7 days without washing my hair and have become a dry shampoo addict! But you know what? When I wash my hair, blow it out and style it, I feel like a million bucks. I walk around with a little more strut in my step. Add a little makeup, slip on a dress, and put my jewelry on... watch out world! Crista is on fire! Taking these little actions makes me feel attractive. What's it for you? What makes you feel sexy, alive and hot?

Perhaps it's the smell of your freshly washed hair, the feel of that feminine dress on your body, or that matching bra and panty set.

Or when you leave the gym and you are all sweaty but feel strong and happy. Or when you get a massage and after you feel like you are walking on cloud 9.

When you start to explore and discover the actions that make you feel attractive, you break the spell of the "I'm not pretty enough" fairy tale.

When clients work with me, I teach them to create a Pre-date Feminine Ritual. The intention of this ritual is to create the time and space to transition from "work" mode into "alive and attractive" mode and to create a routine of actions that bring out your va va va voom factor.

Take Diane for example. Her Pre-date Feminine Ritual consisted of an aromatic bath, styling her hair, and applying fun makeup and a glittery headband.

She said, "The minute I put on my glittery headband, it's on! I feel so good!"

This is what I want for you. I want you to discover what your "glittery headband" is.

Is it dancing to the *Grease* soundtrack? Rubbing yourself down with your favorite smelling body butter? Sitting in silence in front of a burning candle with Tibetan Bowl music playing in the background? Or perhaps your ritual includes adorning yourself with accessories!

Think about the things that make you glow... just like the moment Fiona kisses Shrek for the first time. She rises up into the air, glowing. Bright light radiates from her, then a shock wave from her body shatters all the windows in the church she is in. Her transformation is complete, and Fiona realizes she is still an ogre. She thought she was supposed to be "beautiful" now, but Shrek tells her that she is beautiful, and they kiss again. She is free from the enchantment, the enchantment of thinking she's unattractive, and finally she can fully embrace all she is.

******

EXERCISE:

It's time to get in tune with your aliveness and discover the feminine rituals that will infuse you with feeling attractive.

Pull out your journal and start to brainstorm all the activities that make you feel good. List everything at first. Use the following questions to inspire your list.

What specific things make you feel pretty?

What activities make you feel grounded and peaceful?

What activities bring out your aliveness?

What things have you been wanting to do, but you have been putting off?

Which type of clothes make you feel attractive? (When you put this on you just light up and wiggle a little bit?)

What smells make you go mmmmmmmmmmm?

What is your favorite color? Do you have any clothes in that color?

What activities make you feel strong and alive?

In what ways do you like to move your body?

What activities make you feel feminine and good?

Ok...now that you have brainstormed all of these things that make you feel good and attractive, go back through your list and circle your top 10.

START TO DO THESE THINGS IN YOUR LIFE!

Now write out your top ten on another page of your journal.

Circle three or four of those things that can be included in your Pre-date Feminine Ritual. Things you can easily do before a date that will help you transition back into the beautiful goddess that you are!

Before you go out on your next date, make sure you schedule in time for your Pre-date Feminine Ritual.

Aliveness is HOT.

CHAPTER RECAP

- You get to decide how attractive you are, how you want to show up, and the level to which you *feel* attractive.
- "Attractive enough" doesn't exist, because no one gets to decide what pretty is as a standard.
- Your level of attractiveness has nothing to do with whether you can have a loving partner or not. Seriously, it doesn't.
- It's time to claim your own attractiveness.
- Creating your Pre-date Feminine Ritual will give you instant access.

Now you know that thinking you're not attractive enough will only get you feeling discouraged and insecure. Taking ownership of how attractive you *feel* on the other hand, will turn heads.

Next it's time to see how to have men approach you, without ever changing who you are...

8

You Don't Meet A Girl Like That in Every Dynasty

"I'm too intimidating."

Over time, the princesses' roles in Disney have changed. They started off as being completely passive or even asleep during the final rescues in Snow White and the Seven Dwarves, Cinderella, and Sleeping Beauty, to assisting the prince in Pocahontas and saving the entire nation of China in Mulan.

"The flower that blooms in adversity is the most rare and beautiful of all." whispered the Emperor to Shang after Mulan walks away.

She just finished fighting on behalf of her feeble father who was called into the army in order to fight the invading Huns. She did this all under the guise of being a man. After cutting her hair and donning the clothing of a warrior, she saves the lives of her fellow soldiers and the Emperor. And with the help of her magic dragon and lucky cricket, she takes down the leader of the Huns. To say she was a badass would be an understatement.

While some men may feel threatened by her new status in the dynasty, the gifts and honors that were bestowed upon her, and her strength and ability to face powerful enemies, Shang can see that Mulan is a gem and that "you don't meet a girl like that in every dynasty."

Shang was attracted to Mulan's strength, determination and accomplishments. While he was not used to being around a woman that was so powerful and successful, this did not stop him from pursuing her.

This leads to another one of the myths and fairy tales told far too often in our culture – the idea that a successful or powerful woman is intimidating.

Let me be clear:

Some men may be intimidated by you, but that does NOT mean you are too intimidating.

Also, just because *some* men may be intimidated by you, does not mean that *all* men are intimidated by you.

Check out these definitions of intimidation:

"Intimidation is intentional behavior that "would cause a person of ordinary sensibilities to fear injury or harm." Wikipedia

"Intimidation" is the name of a criminal offense in several U.S. states.

In·tim·i·date - in'timə,dāt/ - frighten or overawe (someone), especially in order to make them do what one wants.

Given these definitions, calling a woman who is powerful, confident, successful, or any combination of these things "intimidating" is not fitting at all! No wonder women take it as a criticism or as something that's wrong with them when they hear it from a man.

The truth is, when a man is saying this directly to you, he is experiencing fear by being in your presence, and instead of owning it and allowing himself to be vulnerable, he tries to make his experience your fault.

It's true that men may feel intimidated by your looks, your success, your income, your dance moves, your level of education, your sexual prowess... but it is not true that you are intimidating. What is true is that certain men experience feeling nervous or scared around you.

You may have gotten embarrassed, confused, or angry when a man has said this to you. Maybe it's caused you to get in your head and made you think, "What did I do wrong?"

Being labeled with a word like this can feel incredibly frustrating.

But let's take a closer look at why a man may *feel* intimidated.

There's a common misconception among women that men are intimidated by women's achievements. Many women fear that they may be scaring off potential suitors if they become too successful or self-sufficient.

But I can assure you, this is not the case.

A healthy and confident man values a woman with ambition, professional savvy and who can hold her own.

So why has this fairy tale, "I'm too intimidating" been spread around like wildfire?

There are two reasons for this:

First, women often take it to heart when an insecure man dishes this out to them. Instead of seeing this statement as a reflection of the man's own insecurity, many women internalize this and start to judge themselves as being pushy, bossy or self-absorbed.

Second, you may be unintentionally exuding unavailability or unapproachability with your non-verbal communication. It's not that you're being intimidating, it's that you are not sending the signals that you are available to be approached. Instead of running the risk of being rejected, a man will simply refrain from approaching.

One of these reasons is on him. The other reason is on you. But either way, here's what you can do about it:

YOU ARE SUCCESSFUL AS HECK

Perhaps you *are* more successful than he is. After talking to you for a while, he begins to see that you are a professional powerhouse and perhaps even make more than him financially. A lot of people (both male and female) aren't bothered by this dynamic. But of course, there are some men out there who initially, won't want this. Rather than getting caught up in worrying about what a guy will think about your success, consider letting your guard down and allowing him to get to know the real you. If you do this, you'll give him the opportunity to see you as a real person, not just an impressive job title.

There is no reason to downplay or hide your success at all. *Your man will value you.*

Look at Amal and George Clooney. After many years of dating the most beautiful women in Hollywood, the one that knocked his socks off was one of the most impressive and accomplished women on this planet, and he put a ring on it ASAP.

Certain men may be threatened by your intelligence, your social life or your desirability. And in reaction, these men may try to keep you small or try to compete with you. If this is the case, it's on him, not you. He needs to look at what is at play within himself.

Men that react this way usually have low self-worth or feelings of inadequacy. They may even have outdated and undesirable beliefs about women and their "appropriate" role in a relationship. Some men who subscribe to these old-school philosophies even believe it's a woman's job to serve them.

These types of men have not faced their own fears, insecurities, and feelings of abandonment. They haven't done the inner work which would allow them freedom from their irrational fears and in the end, allow them a powerful partnership. Despite where these guys are coming from, your beauty, income, social circle, (or whatever has them feeling small, afraid and not enough) are not things you need to mitigate or apologize for.

Ever. When a man is solid in himself, his woman's talent is his joy, not a threat – and she can rest in his strength and in the peace that her strong man provides.

If a man is intimidated by you and he's trying to undermine you, all it means is that *he is not your man*. Your man will admire you and appreciate your accomplishments… because they make you, you!

It's time to practice putting yourself in circles and situations where you'll meet men who will appreciate your strength, success and power.

Remember – this is where your Dating Compass and your list of places to meet men who are in alignment with what YOU want comes in (see chapters 3 and 5 for more details on this).

Now if a man actually comes out and says "you're too intimidating" remember, *you* are not too intimidating, *he* was having the experience of feeling intimidated.

Imagine if a man said instead, "Wow. After learning all about you I am feeling intimidated. You're so cool. You're so beautiful. And I have a fear that you're just too amazing for someone like me." This is a man who is being vulnerable with what is really going on for him. This, you can work with. Because he's owning his experience and perhaps he will like you so much he'll be up for taking on the inner work required to be a great match for you.

But men who say "You're intimidating" are choosing to put their feelings off on you and to make YOU feel responsible for the inner reaction they are having. Instead of realizing in the moment that they're doing this, you might internalize it and say to yourself, "I'm too intimidating." And suddenly, the comment of a guy who hardly knows you becomes a part of your own inner story and beliefs about yourself.

If this is his attitude, and he's too insecure, then he's right. He is not for you. It would resonate best with you to be with a man who wants to claim you for all that you are. You want a confident man – not an insecure man.

Being with someone who respects and sees you for your fullness is really the only way to create something healthy and lasting. Steer clear of the insecure men of the world.

If a man can't jive with your vibe and runs away, let him run. It just wasn't a good fit.

Believing the fairy tale "I'm too intimidating" can get in the way of you actually having the love you want.

Don't you know some very successful, confident and powerful

women that have incredible careers and lives as well as loving husbands?

If they can, so can you!

According to a study on gender role portrayal in Disney princess movies the "princess was rarely, if ever, seen asserting herself with the prince." Although we can't prove that these portrayals have caused men to believe women should have less power or success than them, it does stand to reason that the movies we all grew up watching had an impact on our belief systems. Or if nothing else, these films reflected the fairy tales society was feeding us.

"The prevalence of domestic work is an important theme in the Disney Princess movies and a substantial change that Disney incorporated over time was the temporary discontinuation of domestic work as a symbol of femininity."

Think about that for a sec... Children watching Disney princess movies were imprinted seeing women doing solely housework, not being ambitious.

"The first three princesses were frequently shown doing domestic work. In Cinderella, the princess did domestic work as an act of submission."

It was not until the "1980s–90s that Disney no longer portrayed the princesses doing domestic work."

Whaatttttt???!!!! Not until the 1990's????

And when these researchers studied all the Disney princess movies, including present day examples, the "gendered messages did not consistently move away from traditional themes in more recent movies."

The research also concluded that "Princess movies may influence a child's gender development."

Yikes!

Perhaps the princess movies are not teaching young men how to interact with a successful and independent woman. When a man is not used to, or skilled in, the ways of wooing smart and successful women, a woman of this caliber may elicit fear in him.

Is it 100% on men that they call women intimidating? Or is this Disney's fault again?

I definitely think Disney has some influence over this behavior.

Check out this observation from the Gender Role Portrayal and the Disney Princesses study:

"The princess always won the love of the prince by the end of the Disney Princess films, and this portrayal of romance provides a strongly gendered message. The child viewer is provided with consistent exposure to the social script that one falls in love either very quickly, at first sight (*Snow White, Sleeping Beauty*), against all odds (*Beauty and the Beast, Mulan, The Princess and the Frog*), or both (*Cinderella, The Little Mermaid, Aladdin, Pocahontas*).

In *Aladdin*, the romance took 2 days to develop, and in *Pocahontas* it developed in 1 day (even though the characters spoke different languages!). In *Beauty and the Beast*, the princess fell in love with a man who arguably was victimizing her. The romance in the two most recent films, *Mulan* and *The Princess and the Frog*, however, developed over time as the characters interacted with each other, often overcoming obstacles together and fostering a friendship as well. This suggests that the more recent Disney Princess movies show a more balanced portrayal of relationship formation."

Whether they fall in love quickly, or they take their time, one thing is clear – these movies have affected our relationship to gender and what is expected from each of them.

ARE YOU COMMUNICATING UNAPPROACHABILITY?

Now let's talk about the piece of this topic you do have control over – the vibe you are putting out.

It takes courage for a man to approach a woman. They're nervous inside and the fear of rejection is always there, but a confident man will do it anyway if he sees an opening. Your job as a single woman looking for love is to communicate approachability, create an opening, and let the man take it from there.

If your facial expression and your walk suggest you have absolutely no interest in talking to others, he might decide it's better to stay away.

Like when Shang brings Mulan's helmet back to her at her family's home. When Mulan sees him, she is warm, inviting and invites him in for dinner with her family. And then from there, he felt like he could explore his attraction to her.

To become even more approachable, consider the subtle messages you're sending with your body language when you're out on the town. Even something as simple as making the effort to throw out a few more smiles really helps.

This brings us back to one of the first lessons I teach all of my clients (which we covered in chapter 5) – make eye contact and smile everywhere they go! When they are in the grocery store: eye contact and smile. When they are on the street: eye contact and smile. When they are walking in their office: eye contact and smile. Practice this with everyone! Practice non-verbally communicating that you are friendly and approachable. (Side note: If someone is creepy, or you get a bad vibe, you don't need to smile at them! Use your best judgement!)

For example, when you're out at a party, talk to the first guy who approaches you. Don't blow him off right away if you aren't attracted or interested; just have a short and pleasant conversation. Other men will be watching how you treat the first man who approaches you. If you are seen as someone who graciously speaks to men who approach you, the other guys nearby will see that you are available to approach.

It's all about communicating approachability.

AM I BEING UNAPPROACHABLE OR IS THIS HIS INSECURITY?

Take Rachel, for example. She said she was getting consistent feedback that "she was intimidating." She was a successful businesswoman who internalized this fairy tale instead of looking at the other person's perspective. She was showing up to dates the same way she would show up to business meetings: to make deals and get things done. She was showing up in a *take charge, let's make this happen* kind of way. She wasn't allowing her tender side to show. She would show up with her interview questions as if she was hiring for her next CFO.

And she wasn't getting second dates with men because of her unconscious approach.

I taught her that when a man goes out on a date, he wants to get away from work mode and wants to enjoy a woman's softness and femininity.

But instead, she was plowing over each of these guys like a bulldozer and not allowing her genuine self to show up.

I encouraged her to put down her guard and enjoy the date as an opportunity to connect with another human being. She did not need to know if he measured up to her long list of demands in a mate. She didn't need to know if he was her future husband. I taught her that all she needed to do was smile, appreciate and listen. She didn't need to drive this deal forward. She needed to relax into herself and create a space between her and these men that invited them to come closer, not repel them.

And guess what? She got more dates! Second dates, and third dates after she made this shift. When I spoke to her recently, she was just about to move into a new home with her life partner!

BREAK THE GLASS SLIPPER FOR
"I'M TOO INTIMIDATING."

How do you break out of the bonds of this particular fairy tale fantasy?

Deciphering the truth of the situation is the only antidote.

When a woman believes the fairy tale that she is intimidating, I notice one strategy she may use is to downplay herself. She downplays her education, income, and level of success just to get guys to like her. But there's no need to do this. *Your* man will want you just the way you are.

If you've resigned yourself to thinking because you're successful, no guy is going to want to be with you, it's time to reset your thinking.

Saying that all guys are shallow, and they would never want to be with a woman as successful as you, is the flip side of this "I'm too intimidating" fairy tale.

Quality men who are looking for a relationship want a woman who has her financial act together and is up to things in life. A quality man wants a woman with her own thriving life. He wants someone he can share life with. When I'm coaching men, I never hear him say, "I just want a woman that's not really up to much in life and who I can just take care of." Not once have I ever heard that from a man. Quality men I speak to want a smart and sharp woman to go on adventures with.

Your man will want you with your level of success, level of intelligence, and level of education. So, if you're showing up fully yourself, open and receptive and a man tells you, "you are intimidating" remember this is *his stuff.*

On the other side of the coin, if you are showing up closed off and unapproachable, it's on you to shift and communicate receptivity and openness.

Don't fall into the swamp of this fairy tale and allow it to lead you into making up untrue stories about yourself or men.

******

EXERCISE:

If you're being told the fairy tale, "you are intimidating" ask yourself, is this *his* own insecurity or am I being unapproachable?

You could ask him directly, "What about me is having you feel intimidated?"

His answer may give you insight into whether he is projecting, or if you're communicating an unwelcoming vibe.

To practice showing up as available and open, smile and make eye contact with one new man a day. Start there, and then move up the scale. When you walk into a room, notice all of the men in the room and acknowledge their presence with your eyes and a smile. Instead of grabbing your phone when you're in a line or in a public place, put your phone away and look around you. Connect with the people around you.

And remember, if a guy is not willing to own his fear and puts it all on you, move on. He's not your guy.

CHAPTER RECAP

- Some men may be intimidated by you, but it does not mean you are intimidating.
- A healthy and confident man values a woman with ambition, professional savvy and who can hold her own.
- If you're showing up closed off and unapproachable you might be scaring men away. It's time to shift and communicate receptivity and openness.

With the knowledge that believing you are too intimidating will only get you resenting men or minimizing your success, you can be free. Deciphering the truth of the situation will give you access to your own inner power to attract a healthy and confident man.

Now it's finally time to learn how to have a great man to commit to you...

9

Don't Commit to Prince Charming Before He Commits to You

"Men Can't Commit."

A wise princess doesn't give away her crown before a suitor has asked for her hand in marriage, oh no. With eyes wide open, she watches how he invests in her, never committing to him before he has committed to her.

Despite what you may see on TV or hear from your friends, not every stereotype about men and commitment is actually true. The more we perpetuate this fairy tale that it's unnatural for a man to commit, the greater harm we do to our dating life and our ability to attract a healthy and successful relationship.

There are a significant number of gender stereotypes when it comes to dating, but a large proportion of them seem to surround heterosexual men and commitment.

Add to the high likelihood that you have probably been burned by a disappearing man at some point, it's easy to believe everything you hear about men playing the field:

"Men don't want to get married."

"Men can't be monogamous."

"Men are just players."

Which leads me to hear a lot of women say…

"I won't be able to find a good man."

"Men are afraid of committing."

"Men are more likely to cheat."

"Men are jerks."

These belief structures, or what I call fairy tales about men and commitment, exist in part because Hollywood perpetuates the idea that desirable men are players.

But are they?

Take James Bond, the epitome of what many men desire to be.

James Bond in the movies embodies the "ideal" of masculinity. Bond in this case is strong, loyal to country, loves women (*lots of women*), (*lots of sexy women*), and sex with lots of women. Thus, he is painted as the "man's man" as well as the man women love to love.

THE BOND STEREOTYPE - THE "IDEAL" OF MASCULINITY

Bond encompasses the fantasies of men as well as the fantasies of women. He is the perfect picture of every stereotype of what masculinity should look like and what it means to be a man. For example – men are not wired for commitment.

Is this stereotype true? NO.

The iconic image of Bond is powerful. It sticks to our brains and impacts how we relate to ALL men.

When it comes to gender stereotypes surrounding dating that are still alive today, the heterosexual male who won't commit is the most false.

The truth is, there are many men who are very happy and faithful in committed relationships – who are even more commitment-oriented than many women.

Separating fact from the fairy tale can help you better navigate the dating world — and maybe even help you take the plunge in your own dating life, opening your heart to love again.

Don't buy into the fairy tale that men don't like commitment, or they don't want to get married, or they can't be monogamous.

MEN ARE ABSOLUTELY WIRED FOR COMMITMENT

Men are amazing human beings who are not only deeply committed, but they thrive in commitment.

A recent study found that there are brain differences between non-monogamous and monogamous men, and that there are *plenty* of men who are unwaveringly committed to their partner. These men seem to actually be neurologically *wired* for commitment. The researchers concluded that an individual's desire to commit may have more to do with brain chemistry than gender.

The label society has given men of being "sex crazed animals that can't commit and are more likely to cheat" is not true.

We've actually found that men commit for largely the same reasons women commit. These reasons are social, emotional and sexual.

Recent research has shown that people's reasons for cheating have more to do with issues that are not resolved in a relationship, or personal motivators, than their personal disposition or gender.

And despite what you may have heard about the biological imperative for men to sleep around, research actually concludes that there's no natural code telling men to sleep with as many partners as they can to increase the likelihood of having offspring that would survive and thrive.

Scientists say that mating strategies depend more on gender ratio. If you find that most men seem to want to just jump from partner to partner with no long-term commitment, perhaps women far outnumber men where you live. Perhaps move to Qatar where the sex ratio is 4 men for every one woman. You would definitely get snatched up quick there!

"But Crista, men *are* afraid of committing! No men want to commit to me."

I'm here to tell you that men are not scared of commitment, they are perhaps scared of committing to the wrong woman. And if you put pressure on a commitment-minded man to commit to you before he is ready, he will probably leave you because he needed more time to make this decision. Because when a man is committed, he is committed.

WHAT MEN REALLY WANT

While some of the single men I talk to do say they're afraid of losing their freedom if they settle down, their reasons are different than you may think. It's not that they're afraid they won't get to sleep with enough women, but rather, it's that they really want to be appreciated, trusted, and respected within their relationship. If they get all these things and they see a future with you, commitment will follow.

The only way to have a man deeply surrender his heart to you is to give him freedom. When you stop trying to control the commitment process and start truly seeing him, he will give you ownership of his heart.

Men want to experience being *received* as men. They want to be able to make a woman deeply happy. This level of connection is liberating for a man. It's freeing for him.

Believing this fairy tale that men can't commit, hurts. And it has many women deeply question, "What's the point of even dating if a man will never be loyal, steadfast, or in it for the long haul?"

But here's what I want you to seriously consider...

MEN HAVE A DIFFERENT TIMELINE FOR COMMITMENT THAN WOMEN

In my years of studying women in the dating process I have found that many women have a certain timeline of how they think commitment is supposed to look. In general, this timeline can be faster than that of most men which can lead many women to fall into the trap of pushing the relationship towards commitment before a man is ready.

Have you ever had an amazing first date and found yourself trying on his last name before you really know if there's long-term potential? Heck, you may meet a man at the bus stop, and you try on his last name!

Maybe you can guess by now where we've gotten the belief that commitment should happen so fast?... That's right, it's another Disney movie classic plot. The main characters fall in love within seconds and spend the rest of their lives together... so it's not your fault if you think commitment should move faster than it does.

From my observation of men, commitment is a duty. It's an obligation. And they honor this commitment and are responsible to this commitment. If this is the standard they hold themselves to, it makes sense that men would take a little longer perhaps to make a commitment, especially if they're a high-quality man.

The mistake I see a lot of women making is expecting that exclusivity needs to happen right away in order to feel special or to take a man seriously as a long-term potential. Instead of being easy going in the beginning stages of getting to know a man, a woman might try to lock down the commitment.

I spoke to a single woman recently who actually had a fantastic budding relationship with a great guy. They were dating for a few months and they had a wonderful time together and a lovely connection. He was definitely interested in her.

He had just gotten divorced a couple of years ago. He had 2 kids that he shared custody with, and he was still adjusting to being a single dad and healing from the ending of his last relationship. He was a quality guy. He wasn't rushing into anything, and he was taking his time. She took it personally when he didn't want to introduce her to his kids right away. She got upset when he wasn't asking her to be his girlfriend. She was showing up as anxious, super eager and demanding. She had these expectations that a commitment on some level needed to happen.

When a woman shows up this way, it can really scare a man off. He may actually care for her and be seriously considering her for a long-term relationship, but because she's pressuring him before he's ready, he will disappear. She's forcing his hand at this point. When you do this, he will most likely let you go because he has not collected enough information about you and your connection to make a commitment to you. So, if he's forced to choose, he will let you go.

Like I said earlier, a man wants to be received by you, not pressured by you.

DON'T COMMIT TO HIM BEFORE HE COMMITS TO YOU

Another mistake women make is to attach too quickly to a man before he has attached or committed to her.

Many women have a strong desire to have the experience of someone committing to them. This desire can lead them to push a relationship along before taking the time to get to know him and assess if he is truly into her. Also, many women assume that men have the same timeline as them.

A high-quality man makes commitments. He's not going to over promise and under deliver. If he commits to something, he's going to do it. He's responsible. He is a man of his word.

High quality men are often actually really slow to commit because they want to make sure they're committing to the right person for them and not just committing in the moment. They really put some thought into it.

So instead of pushing a commitment, allow a man some space and watch how he is showing up in your life.

According to Barbara De Angelis' book, *Secrets About Men Every Woman Should Know*, women have a natural tendency to fill in the gap if we feel there is one. Sometimes we tend to think that we have to DO something in order to get a man to love us. To compensate for this, we become givers and try to fill in the emotional gaps.

Especially when you're initially dating, you need to give men the chance to find out how they really feel about you. You can't rush this.

If you're so busy trying to sell yourself to a man, you're not creating a space for him to want you on his own.

We as women have a picture in our mind of what a good relationship should look like, and so we find a man and go about creating that relationship without much participation on his part.

It's like we say, "You show up every day, and I'll take care of the emotional part of the relationship. I'll create the intimacy, the social activities, the conversations, and the direction. All you have to do is be my partner."

The danger in doing this is that we often end up practically being in a relationship with ourselves. It's like being in a two-person kayak and you are the only one rowing! You are a one-woman rowing machine!

According to De Angelis, there are ways women fill in the gap:

Social

Sexual

Intimacy

Communication

Creative

When you start out dating someone and you're filling in all the blanks by taking all the initiative, you feel happy and think that you are indeed in a relationship. But then, after some time, you will get resentful when you realize you are the only one carrying the relationship.

It's imperative to leave room for a man to fill in the blanks himself.

You need to give a man a chance to fill in the gaps between you.

Men feel good about themselves when they take charge or initiate action.

When you take initiative and fill in all the blanks, you deny this man the opportunity to learn more about loving you.

And if you fill in the blanks, and you're the only one initiating connection during the beginning stages of a relationship, you run the risk of deluding yourself into believing you are in a committed relationship.

There are many reasons why you might continually initiate connection and try to fill up the gap between you and a man.

Perhaps you may feel like you have to earn love, or that the relationship will fall apart if you don't fill in the gaps.

So, give the men you are dating the opportunity to fill in the space between you.

Stop pursuing a man after you initially connect with him.

Focus instead on making a reflection connection and reflect his level of investment.

I encourage my female clients who are dating men to reflect

what he does.

One of two things will happen when you stop initiating/pursuing….

1. The man will rise to the occasion and start connecting with you
2. The man's true non-involvement and non-interest in the relationship will be revealed, and he will disappear.

That's why I encourage my clients who are in the beginning stages of dating to receive. Graciously receive. Allow him to fill in the space and see where he leads you. Receive.

I find that many women jump "into a relationship" with a man – asking him out, sleeping over, talking all the time on the phone, etc. – but then he leaves her out of the blue and she realizes she was the only one in the "relationship." It was not a relationship at all. It was just one woman who wanted a relationship with a certain man, and she was the only one paddling the boat, so to speak.

This usually happens when women have put all their eggs in one man's basket before he has even communicated that he wants to commit to her.

That's why I recommend "giving space" between you and

the men you're dating. Allow space for him to pursue you. Allow him to show up for you. If you're doing all of the social planning, initiating the intimacy, connecting through texts, and all of the pursuing and you don't allow any space to be there for him to show up, you'll never know if he is really into you or not.

Mirror his level of investment and don't jump ahead of him.

Keep getting to know other men and only commit to one when you and the man you like have had a conversation around exclusivity.

A man is your boyfriend when the two of you are exclusive and both of you are not seeing anyone else. This may take 1 month, 3 months or 6 months. This happens over a conversation that he initiates.

"What? Why should I let him initiate this?"

If you find that you feel an anxiety within yourself to have "the talk" with him, a "where is this going" talk, you may be investing in the relationship more than he is, or you may have committed to him emotionally before he has to you.

If you find that you're starting to want to nail down where this relationship is going, instead, get busy connecting with and staying open to other men.

Because remember, no man is your boyfriend until you are exclusive. It may take some patience on your part, to allow yourself to not know where it is going in the beginning stages of dating.

CONSIDER SAVING YOUR EXCLUSIVITY BENEFITS FOR YOUR FUTURE BOYFRIEND WHO HAS COMMITTED TO YOU, NOT EVERY MAN YOU START DATING

I also teach women to not give away all of their "Exclusivity Benefits" before a man has committed and is even her boyfriend.

"Exclusivity Benefits" include extended quality time, intimate physical affection, romantic gifts, resource-intensive personal favors, girlfriend-like emotional support, and sex.

It's a benefit to be in your feminine presence and when you extend these gifts to a man before he has even invested in you in a similar way, you are getting ahead of him in his commitment process as well as acting like his girlfriend when he hasn't even requested it yet.

Here are some more detailed examples of Exclusivity Benefits:

Extended quality time - Spending the entire weekend

together after you first meet.

Intimate physical affection - Extended snuggle sessions, sleeping over.

Romantic gifts - Giving thoughtful gifts - hearing him say he always wanted to see a band perform, and you buy him a pair of tickets.

Resource-intensive personal favors - Helping him clean his car or driving two hours to pick him up from the airport.

Girlfriend-like emotional support - Spending hours on the phone with him to listen, help, and support him through his recent fight with his sister.

Sex - Having sex before you are exclusive, going over to his house to be physical when he texts you late at night, booty calls.

I find that many women feel most "safe" when they are having sex with a man they are exclusive with. But what happens is that many women are having sex with men way before he has ever discussed being exclusive with her. In an attempt to create the safety that she wants to feel, she tries to secure the commitment by initiating the conversation of 'where is this going'. If you are not the kind of person who is ok with having sex with someone who is also having sex with other people as they are dating you, then wait for exclusivity.

If you're giving away all the Exclusivity Benefits before you're even in an exclusive relationship, you may think you are in a committed relationship simply because you're acting like his girlfriend. But a man is not your boyfriend until the two of you have a conversation about it and you both decide to be exclusive.

Giving away all of the benefits of being with you before he has fully invested in you, is a big mistake many women fall into. Don't assume that because *you* have committed to *him* and you're giving away all the benefits of being with you, that you deserve a commitment from him. This will only make you feel frustrated and confused – and will potentially scare a quality man away.

The reason you're trying to own a man, or trying to secure a commitment early on, is most likely due to the fact that you have committed to him before he has committed to you. That's why I recommend not getting ahead of a man's pace for commitment, saving your Exclusivity Benefits for when you are in a relationship, continuing to date other men, and only committing to a man when he has requested it. Until then, he is not your boyfriend.

Do you want to know when a man will commit to you? When you take the time to really see him, and not simply as a means to fulfill your desire for a committed relationship. When you give him space to get to know you and space to consistently show up for you, then, and only then, will a quality man commit. A man will commit when he is ready.

 ## BREAK THE GLASS SLIPPER FOR
"MEN CAN'T COMMIT."

How do you break out of the bonds of this particular fairy tale fantasy?

Instead of trying so hard to get a commitment from a man, step into being the Queen.

Being the Queen is the only antidote.

What is being the Queen? When you're standing in being Queen the world opens up all of its bountiful blessings to you. All good things come to you. You are a brilliant feminine presence who sits on her throne. Suitors approach her. She never chases suitors. The suitors make effort to approach. As the Queen, your light and warm energy is captivating, and when men see you, they are drawn to you.

A Queen leans back into her throne and is relaxed. She values herself and others value her as well. She does not allow offerings from suitors that do not affirm her queenship. That do not affirm her royal value. She allows men to approach her on the throne and she does so with kindness.

As the Queen, she knows that all good men will be drawn to her because she has what they are looking for: the mysterious light of femininity. She brings sensuality, connection, appreciation, and warmth. She knows her profound value. She is the Queen and she is irresistible.

A Queen does not share her Kingdom with any suitor that comes her way. She entertains them, gets to know them, sees what they offer and provide consistently, and sees which ones ask for her hand in marriage. She has multiple suitors that want to relish in her femininity, and she knows her value.

******

EXERCISE:

Make a reflection connection.

After contact has been initiated with a man, learn to create a reflection connection. Reflect his level of investment and don't get ahead of him in the commitment process.

Practice allowing the space for a man to initiate and pursue you and reflect back to him his efforts. His offerings.

For example, if he sends you a text, text him back...something of similar length. (reflection connection).

If he asks you out for a date, say yes (if you like him).

If he calls you, call him back.

If he shares something intimate about himself, share something about yourself (but keep it light, you don't want to dump all of your deep baggage during the beginning stages of a relationship)

If he kisses you, kiss him back.

In the beginning phases of dating allow space for him to fill the gap. And then graciously receive his efforts.

And when you are interacting with him, whether it is texting, calling, or on a date, keep things light, easy and fun.

This is one of the only ways I know that will help you to know if a man is truly into you or not, and to cultivate a light atmosphere to connect with you and to ultimately want to commit to you.

As a woman looking for a long-term committed relationship, the only options you should seriously consider in the first few dates, are the men who are pursuing you without you having to invest your Exclusivity Benefits. Once you invest your Exclusivity Benefits you won't know if he is truly interested in you, or the benefits.

Practice making a reflection connection.

CHAPTER RECAP

- Men have a different timeline for commitment than women. When you understand this, you will save yourself a lot of grief.
- Don't commit to a man before he has committed to you. Keep your options open and create many connections with amazing men.
- Until the two of you have had a conversation about exclusivity, a man is not your boyfriend. So, stop acting like he is.
- Reflect his level of investment and allow the man you are dating the time and space to truly determine how he really feels about you.

Now that you know that getting ahead of a man in the commitment process can actually push a high-quality man away, you can create a new pattern. Creating a reflection connection will allow you to see where you stand with a man and move at a healthy pace.

For our final chapter, let's talk about how to create confidence (the most attractive quality to a man) and to own yourself in your skin...

10

Mirror, Mirror, On the Wall, Who's the Thinnest of Them All?

"I'm too overweight to be loved"

The mirror has played tricks with so many unfortunate women before you, making them believe that every crack and crevice and smudge belonged to their body. This mirror is part of a magic trick, smoke and mirrors, trap doors and cards, and has more tricks up its sleeve for you, until you realize that you're you, and not what the mirror portrays.

"I love your body."

This was the moment Norma's healing began. She deeply needed to hear those words and the Universe provided them through Robert, a man who claimed that she was the woman he had always dreamed of.

She thought to herself, "What's wrong with this man? Does he not seek perfection?"

You see, over the years with Juan, Norma had tried everything to lose weight. Diet, exercise, cleanses, everything. She believed the fairy tale, "I'm too overweight to be lovable."

And because of this fairy tale she wasted 5 years of her life with Juan, a man she met on the dance floor in a salsa club. He was handsome, a great dancer, and had a sexy engineer's mind. When she first saw him, she thought, "He's mine!"

"I normally don't date women like you. You're a little bit too big for the type of women I like," he said.

Instead of walking away from Juan that very instant, she said, "That's ok. I can lose the weight."

She then quickly proceeded to turn the tables on him and said, "I don't normally date men with children, but I'll give you an opportunity to be with me."

And from there the tug of war began.

She became obsessed with looking for ways to be better – the better version of Norma. She would work out 2 hours a day, surround herself with personal trainers, and when she would lose 5 to 10 pounds, Juan did treat her a little differently. She even participated in one of those physique body shows for motivation, but it still wasn't enough, and Juan told her, "You can do better."

After investing 5 years of her life with this man, she couldn't do enough to keep him happy with her body. Norma desperately wanted to be in a relationship and wanted to make it work, but this obsession with losing weight really started to do a number on her psyche.

She grasped onto meditation and began the journey to still her mind and go within. She saw Juan as a broken man who needed her. It was much easier for Norma to focus on taking care of him, instead of herself. Juan was not loving her, but more importantly, she was not loving herself.

"It was a 'me' against 'me' situation," Norma said. And it was time for her to win.

It wasn't until she realized she had to love herself that she was able to set herself free from this relationship and declare, "I'm done with this."

When he came home from work, she told him that she was going to Dallas.

"Oh. Is that so? Did you clean the house? Did you cook

something for me?"

"Yes."

"When are you coming back?"

"Never…. It's selfish of me to continue asking you to do something I haven't been willing to do for myself – to love me."

And then she walked out the door.

She began a two-year healing journey, to love her body, and listen to her inner voice.

She got to a place where she was able to silence her mind long enough to hear the woman within who says, "I love you. I am here for you."

From this beautiful centered place within herself, she met Robert. What was meant to only be a quick dinner date turned into 3 hours, and within 3 months turned exclusive. Now they've been together for two years, making plans for marriage and merging their lives.

Now when Robert says the words, "I love your body," Norma can *receive* them because the fairy tale – "I'm too overweight to be loved" lost its spell over her.

But there are many people today who suffer from this spell and believe they are too overweight to date or to find love.

I hear:

"When I lose 20 pounds I will start to date again."

"I don't want anyone to see my body naked!"

"No one will want me the weight that I am."

And because of these thoughts they don't allow themselves to have love in their lives.

Why have we so deeply believed this fairy tale? Because we haven't realized that we've been looking into a broken mirror, not a polished one. This deceptive and broken mirror makes us believe that every chip, crack, and speck of dirt belongs to our body and face, but it really belongs to the mirror. It's dark magic.

Hollywood is this broken mirror, for the only characters that are worthy of love on screen are thinner than average.

Even beautiful movie stars like Jennifer Lawrence have been told that they are overweight. In an interview she said, "Somebody told me I was fat, that I was going to get fired if I didn't lose a certain amount of weight. They brought in pictures of me where I was basically naked and told me to use them as motivation for my diet."

The "right" shape and size continue to dominate popular media.

And not only do most movies, TV shows and ads mainly feature thin women, they've also set the narrative that if you're bigger than the approved shape and size, you need to be trying to lose weight.

Take the Emmy-nominated show, *This Is Us*, which features Chrissy Metz who plays the character Kate, who's story revolves largely around her misery over her weight.

Weight loss drives Kate's decisions throughout the show and she personifies this problematic narrative in Hollywood that in order for a main character of size to be worthy of love, attention, and a relationship — she needs to want and be trying to lose weight.

But in real life, Metz doesn't focus on the numbers. She focuses on how she feels. On a radio show she said she didn't find true self-acceptance until she stripped down and sang to her naked self in the mirror.

Her vocal coach told her, "Chrissy, I want you to sing in the mirror naked."

Metz was like, "The hell? You want me to what?"

But she gave her coach's suggestion a shot, and her mindset completely changed.

Metz explained how singing in the nude while looking at her reflection changed the way she viewed her body.

"It's just accepting you're not your body. It's the vessel that your spirit occupies," Metz said.

But how do you go from hating your body to loving it?

Do we have to hit our head like Renee from the film *I Feel Pretty*? (If it were only that easy!)

Renee, a woman who has deep insecurities and low self-esteem, and considers herself overweight, awakens from a brutal fall in an exercise class believing she is the most beautiful, capable, model-like woman on the planet.

During the film, before Renee's big change, she would spend a few minutes in the mirror each night looking at her body, being disappointed. She hated her curves as she peeled the Spanx off her body. This movie takes a big magnifying glass to the inside of this woman's insecure mind and the fact that Hollywood and the "beauty" industry plays a large part in women feeling bad about their bodies.

A painful part of the film for me was seeing how Renee would love to have a man in her life, but deep down she thought she was too overweight and that no guy would want her just the way she was. This was painful to watch because I come across so many single women like Renee.

The beauty of the film was seeing this once insecure woman, find her confidence and live her life fearlessly.

I am worthy of love, exactly how I am.

Because Renee's perspective changed, all she saw was beauty reflected back to her when she looked in the mirror. She walked with a bounce in her step, saw the world in a whole new way, and in this space of confidence – attracted the loveliest man who loved all of her.

And that's what I am pointing to in this chapter, your perspective on how you have allowed Hollywood to influence how you see yourself, your weight, and your body.

This faulty messaging from Hollywood does not just stay on the screen, it permeates our minds and hearts, influences our actions, and for many women it can cause prolonged inaction in their love lives.

"I'm too overweight to be loved" is a made-up story that stops many women from getting out there and getting what they truly want, a loving and supportive relationship with a great person.

Sheila was a 34-year-old single woman who came to me for dating support. She was lovely, intelligent, had a great job in New York, and a loving family. Eight years ago, she had a boyfriend and when things ended with him, she never felt closure. She had not dated since.

She hired me because she knew something had to change. She was tired of being alone. Another interesting element to this story is that Sheila had a twin sister with whom she spent almost all of her time.

But recently, Sheila's twin sister had found a boyfriend and was building her life with him. So naturally, she started shifting her focus away from Sheila and onto her relationship with this new man. Sheila painfully started to feel this huge void in her life. Her sister was the person she would go out to dinner with, go to the movies with, and spend her free time around. So, when her sister started spending time with this new man, Sheila started feeling more alone than ever.

When I asked her what she felt was sabotaging her ability to be in the relationship that she wanted, she said, "I'm too overweight. Every time I look in the mirror, I can't help but see that I'm fat."

I said, "Well, how much do you weigh?" After she told me her actual weight, I asked her if she knew women her weight who were in a relationship or married? She said yes. I told her that I have also seen women her weight in loving relationships.

For 8 years, this fairy tale, this idea that Sheila was too heavy at the moment, had been spinning around in her mind and lying to her... telling her she wasn't good enough for love.

After talking things out on that initial phone call with Sheila, she had a realization... the reason she hadn't found love was not her weight, but rather because she wasn't putting herself out there. She finally saw that she had bought into the fairy tale society had been telling her, that Hollywood had been telling her, and that she was telling herself.

After a while, believing "I'm too overweight" as the main reason love hasn't happened for you, becomes an excuse. It's a way for your mind to justify why you're still single and it also can prevent you from taking action. It's like a two-edged sword. Once you believe this fairy tale, it's almost impossible to find love because you feel so much shame around your body that you just want to hide. How can you feel inspired to authentically date when you think there is something wrong with you?

FACT: Your weight has nothing to do with your ability to find love.

I am so surprised by all the women who tell me that they need to lose weight first before they start dating again. They could be 120 pounds, 140 pounds, 170 pounds, 195 pounds, 260 pounds. It doesn't actually matter what their weight is. If a woman thinks she is overweight, then it stops her from feeling good about herself and from taking action in her love life.

Take Tania for example. She's a 35-year-old single mother who, after her child was born, felt extremely unattractive. She absolutely hated her thighs, thinking they were too big. Plus, add the fact that she was not getting along well with her son's father, she got into a rut and felt miserable.

But she got sick and tired of feeling bad about her body, so she started to change her mindset. She would meditate and read books that would uplift her life. She would take seminars to help bring her life to the next level, which included radical self-love. She put in effort to change her mindset, and she has transformed herself into a juicy, eye-catching goddess.

Now, by Hollywood standards, Tania would be considered overweight. She still has a belly left over from childbearing and is 5′4″. But boy does she know how to work those curves!

When Tania walks into a room now, all heads turn. I mean ALL heads, men and women. She is like a magnet. Her flowing hair, her charming Mona Lisa smile, her makeup done in the most natural and lovely way, her classy fitted dress and high heels make everyone wonder who she is. Feminine freedom is the best way to describe her when she walks in the room. She flows. She almost sparkles. Her self-confidence is what makes her so sexy. Sexiness oozes out of her. She takes massive action on the dating scene, too. She goes out with strong, attractive, sexy men. Rich men love her. Young men love her. Older men love her. She owns her body; she radiates aliveness and people melt in her presence. It's powerful.

Tania threw away the fairy tale of thinking that her thighs were too big, and now men are fawning over her left and right.

Just like Tania, our bodies change. Our bodies change when we have a baby, when we gain weight, when our metabolism slows down, when we stop being active, when we age, etc. And hey, you may not feel like you used to and that can feel frustrating and be hard to adjust to.

Even though your body feels different, remember you are your worst critic!

And remember, there are men who are attracted to all types of bodies. If there's one thing you can learn from the various real-life stories in this chapter, it's that nothing makes a woman sexier than her confidence and her ability to love herself. You want to create a loving relationship with a man who will appreciate you in all of your stages and forms.

Thinking you have to lose weight before you date is a trap you can get stuck in…. forever.

Here's the pattern I see over and over again with single women: When women feel bad about themselves, they give up and lose hope. Without any hope, they get resigned and take no action in their love lives. Without action, there will be no possibility of love. Many people internalize this fairy tale to the point where they don't even bother dating!

Don't wait until you are 20 pounds lighter because you know how losing weight goes – sometimes you lose it, sometimes you don't.

Instead...

BREAK THE GLASS SLIPPER FOR
"I'M TOO OVERWEIGHT"

How do you break out of the bonds of this particular fairy tale fantasy?

Break the spell of the magic mirror by realizing that it is broken, not you.

It's time to look deeply into your eyes through this cracked mirror and tell yourself, "You are not broken. You are worth something beautiful."

The only thing not worth a dime is this broken mirror you have been looking into, for it has been a con artist duping you, as with so many other victims before you. It will pull the wool over your eyes every time you forget about its dubious nature.

This mirror will try to take over you and scar your body and mind by making you think that false statements are true. Go and grab your magic sword and break every crack in that mirror into pieces.

It's time to expose the lies of this broken mirror and realize that you are you, and not what it depicts. You're a beautiful woman who will polish not only her own mirror, but the mirror of others as well.

******

EXERCISE:

Just like Chrissy Metz, sing and dance in the mirror naked. That's the exercise. Put on your favorite song, strip down, and own it! Do this until you're no longer uncomfortable. Do this until you are fully having fun and loving your body again.

Radical self-love is the only way to break the mirror.

CHAPTER RECAP

- The "right" shape and size continue to dominate popular media, but your weight has nothing to do with your ability to find love.

- Thinking you have to lose weight before you date is a trap that you can get stuck in…. forever.

- Don't wait until you are 20 pounds lighter before you start to date because you know how losing weight goes – sometimes you lose it, sometimes you don't.

- Radical self-love is the only antidote, so learn how to have fun and feel good in your body.

Now you know that the broken mirror will dupe you into thinking you have to lose weight before you find love. So, it's time to change your mindset and transform yourself into a juicy eye-catching goddess.

To finish off, take some time to reflect on what's next now that you have discovered the top ten fairy tales that sabotage your chances at finding love....

The End

"What's next?"

Now that you know each of the fairy tales, it's time to break the glass slipper for each and every last one of them!

Over the years of being in the coaching industry, I find that people can only absorb and apply a few things at once into their lives. Let's take this time as an opportunity to think about which fairy tales you are ready to let go of.

Now that you've read this book in its entirety, you know that love can happen for you when you put yourself out there and take action – instead of believing that love will just magically happen on its own. You can now tell whether a man is in alignment with you and your core values by using your Dating Compass to sort, instead of using chemistry or your "type" of man to screen out the best relationship for you.

You will now honor your feelings, heal your past, and open your heart to love again. You will no longer keep yourself busy and distracted from what you truly want in your heart – to find companionship and someone to spend the rest of your life with.

Your eyes are opened, and on the lookout for a GOOD man, a commitment-minded man… and you're now willing to take the risk and put yourself out there to connect with him. No longer will you let the number of years you have been on this planet stop you from claiming what is rightfully yours – a quality person to share your life with. Your weight, your looks, or how successful you are, will no longer hinder the Queen within you who powerfully claims the life that SHE wants.

I distinguished a lot of fairy tales in this book, and it would be unrealistic to expect that you can immediately stop believing each and every one of them on the spot. Many of these fairy tales could potentially be wrapped up in your identity and lifestyle and change like that takes time.

Take a moment right now, review each of the fairy tales, and choose a few that you most need to release.

Have you chosen them? Ok…now…

Picture each of these fairy tales as a glass slipper – lined up on a waist-high stone wall in front of YOUR castle.

These slippers are laid out for you in the sunlight. This book is the hammer, and I am giving you permission to smash each and every one of them.

I cannot break them for you. You must be willing to break them for yourself.

And now is the time. No more just reading words in a book and moving on with your life. It's TIME to shake things up and take action.

It's time to break the illusions that have been getting in the way of your happiness and fulfillment in life.

You have two choices at this moment. It's like the scene in *The Matrix* when Morpheus asks Neo to choose between the red pill and the blue pill. You can continue to live in the illusion of your own personal fairy tale, OR you can live in reality.

It's time to break the glass slipper.

Once a slipper is broken and shattered into a million pieces, there is no going back.

The opportunity to destroy the stories in your mind that prevent you from the love you so desperately want is before you.

These fairy tales have acted like a fence around your mind,

limiting what's possible in your love life.

As the Queen, you will no longer chase men who offer crumbs. Oh no! You are a Queen!

It's time to claim who you are. It's time to claim the gifts that you have to share with your future man.

From this day forth, you are on a journey. You are rewriting YOUR love story. Dating to find your true love is a spiritual journey. This is a journey in which you must face yourself and your fears and take action, regardless of any resistance you may experience.

This can be a tremendously intimate quest that will definitely, and most completely, deepen your insight into your true self and your life. This isn't about finding a man, just any man, for relationship sake. This is NOT about checking off that box in life. This is an opportunity for you to claim yourself, your values, your needs, your vision of the future, and to find someone in alignment with THAT.

This is more than just partnering up with someone. This is about partnering up with your true self. You get to decide from this moment forward that you will no longer be a woman who sweeps things under the rug by ignoring your feelings or needs, just to feel some temporary sense of security.

When you are the Queen of your love life, you create the security within yourself. You protect your kingdom. You protect your heart. You now honor what you desire and need in your life.

Instead of seeing dating as a pain in the butt, or some exhausting thing that feels like work, start to see it as an avenue to find deeper understanding of yourself, and as a pathway to build muscles of your own inner strength.

Dating is a fantastic opportunity to let go of the past and to just stop worrying about the future.

You do not learn by staying in your comfort zone. You learn and grow when you leave the metaphorical safety that these fairy tales provide and deal head-on with the challenges – in reality – that you are confronted with.

Everyone's journey towards love is unique.

I invite you to consider dating as a spiritual journey. After all, isn't life itself a voyage in one way or another?

> *"We are not human beings having a spiritual experience.*
> *We are spiritual beings having a human experience."*
>
> ~ *Pierre Teilhard de Chardin*

Whether or not you agree that dating with the intention to find love is a spiritual journey, what is important is that you have the right tools to make the most out of your quest for love.

There are certain steps and tools you can rely on to make the journey as easy and fruitful as possible (for example, hiring a dating coach, like me, might come in handy).

Reading this book was also a great first step on embarking on a quest to deepen your knowledge, understanding, and wisdom about yourself and the world and paradigms you were born into. I'm inviting you to join me on this journey to purposely lead an intentional and conscious lifestyle in order to gain insights about yourself and your life – and to truly attract the partner of your dreams.

For this book's sake, I made Hollywood the enemy. But who is really the true enemy? It's easy to blame others for your own life, but the warrior's true journey is to take ownership of her life, the choices she has made, and the paradigms she has chosen to buy into that no longer serve her.

To walk the path of intentionally and consciously finding love, you need to start with the main question:

"Where do I want to go?"

Seriously… where do you want to go?

Not many people take the time to truly think this through.

As you've discovered in this book, people think love is just some magical thing that will happen when they least expect it. But the truly wise take the time to consider what they want in their heart of hearts and in their lives – beyond the constraints society has placed on them.

This is all about having the courage to embark on a journey that YOU want.

Soooo... I ask you....

WHAT do YOU want?

If you sincerely want the companionship, security, and experience of deep love with an amazing man, then it's time to own the warrior within you, the Queen within you, and make this happen.

My goal of this book was to expose any of the security blankets that you've had in place that prevent you from experiencing the love that you so rightfully have access to. It's time to break your glass slipper and free yourself of the fairy tale fantasies that no longer serve you and find true love in real life

About the Author

CRISTA BECK, known as "The Love Radar," has been a featured expert on ABC, NBC, FOX, and TEDx. Her message has been heard by over a million people globally. With over 20,000 hours of meditation as well as an award-winning violinist, Crista brings pure love to her 10+ years as a love & dating coach.

To find out more about upcoming events, workshops, and to create your own powerful Dating Compass, head to *breaktheglassslipper.com.*

Made in the USA
Middletown, DE
16 November 2019

78648480R00125